CASES AND VIEWS FROM A GENERAL PRACTITIONER IN INDUSTRIAL/ORGANIZATIONAL PSYCHOLOGY

by

Clyde C. Mayo, Ph.D.

DORRANCE
PUBLISHING CO
EST. 1920
PITTSBURGH, PENNSYLVANIA 15238

Dorrance Publishing Co
585 Alpha Drive
Pittsburgh, PA 15238
Visit our website at *www.dorrancebookstore.com*

ISBN: 978-1-4809-3807-6
eISBN: 978-1-4809-3784-0

Contents

LIST OF TABLES

LIST OF EXHIBITS

BOOK DEDICATED TO
(In alphabetical order)

Dana Glenn Dunleavy PhD, Senior Psychologist for the Medical College Admission Program (MCAT)

David Finley PhD, Vice-President of Human Resources, Ingram-Micro, Inc., Independent Consultant

Cheryl Frankeny PhD, Owner of Management and Personnel Systems, LLC

Joan Glaman PhD, Senior Psychologist at Boeing, Inc.

Milton D. Hakel, PhD President, SIOP Foundation

Patrick McNiel PhD, Director of Psychological Services, Houston Police and Fire Departments

Betty Sue G. Thompson PhD (deceased), Director of Organizational Development for the Southland Corporation, Independent Consultant

Darvin Winick PhD, Founder of LWFW, Inc., Independent Consultant

Editors
Rich Arvey, PhD
Joe Baucum, M.S.
Michael Campion, PhD
Ashley Eades, B.S.
Milton D. Hakel, PhD
David Finley, PhD
Mark Friedman, PhD

PROLOGUE

Persons assisting the author in producing this publication are to be thanked and are listed at the bottom of the previous page. Also there is a list of persons to whom the book is dedicated. All are very good psychologists and come from the practitioner, academic, and managerial ranks.

A curious reader would wish to know the coverage of a book plus why it was written. This book will cover selected topics and cases within or related to the field of Industrial/Organizational Psychology. This field deals with the work life of persons in organizations; it parallels, but is not the same as, clinical psychology, which deals with individuals rather than organizations. School psychology deals with the lives of youngsters in an academic environment.

Within each of the fields mentioned above, there are various theories, techniques, and points of view. All of the fields fall within the general discipline of applied psychology, which is called a science by some and an art by others and perhaps a "mixture" of the two by still others.

Target Audience of the Book

Although the author encourages curious outsiders to read it, the book is intended primarily for doctorate level psychologists or advanced master's level I/O people. Certainly it is not intended to be a "handbook" for bachelor's level people to do project design or to substitute experience for a combination of education and experience. A bachelor's level person, although they are certainly welcome to read the book, has not had the exposure to design, develop, and execute projects. To offer an example, the author is familiar with a firm that uses bachelor's level personnel to administer "change management" projects. They travel from organization to organization with a memorized approach complete with questionnaires, training programs, and structured problem-solving devices that are derived from a central figure (the designer). They are not equipped to handle objections, critiques, deviations, or theoretical problems in change management. They are "installers" of a process that doesn't really work in an A-B-C manner. Their input consists of scheduling scoring, and administering standardized sessions to people who "need" to change themselves and their organizations. Master's level personnel are better at project work but must be supervised. For example, a master's level person is usually aware of how to construct a psychological scale but may not understand how the underlying concepts are based on the psychology of perception. The same individual may be able to select and interpret personality tests but may be relatively unaware of the constructs that were accepted/rejected in the effort to put the test together.

There is a tendency in the more commercial firms to select persons to handle sales, client relations, and perhaps some form of interviewing because they have good verbal and interpersonal skills. Such skills are needed in psychologists but they do not substitute for a full set of professional skills.

It should be mentioned that even fully developed professionals are not always correct in their determinations. Their "batting averages" are higher, however, and the amount of professional preparation in which they engage serves as an indicator of dedication to the field.

Why the Book Was Written
The answer to why the book was written will be presented in more detail in the following chapters. For now, the reader will be exposed to how the author "felt" about taking on the project. In the first place, organizations in our culture are becoming larger and more important. They include corporations, civilian groups, national charities, the military, etc. Most are becoming larger; corporations, through mergers and acquisitions as well as other means, are growing by leaps and bounds. Whether and for whom this is good should be examined; I/O psychology can do more to evaluate growth as well as facilitate it.

A variety of techniques to increase organizational productivity or to solve organizational problems have been created by both practitioners and academicians. Selfishly, the author would like those to which he has contributed to be available to other I/O psychologists. Also he would like to share perspectives on the practice. For example, some practitioners and academicians have become "mechanical" in their approach—perhaps because they have been trained to be quantitative as opposed to qualitative in nature.

I/O Psychology is a fertile field which can improve employee morale, reduce conflict, improve productivity, increase the quality of new hires and supervisory promotions, and increase the quality of management. Used wisely, it can benefit society and social organizations. The book will cover both proper and improper use of I/O Psychology as a discipline, as is seen by the author. The author/writer refers to himself as the "author," an "I/O psychologist," and a "consultant" throughout the book. It should not be difficult for the reader to understand that the writer is referred to by these different denotations.

The book is an attempt to offer I/O professionals a head start in their early careers (apprentice level), while also offering journeymen with more experience of new and reconstructed ways of conducting projects. It is an attempt to outline the benefits of using a general practice model. It shows how the "art" of practice can be blended with the "science," using a "holistic" point of view and a technical perspective at the same time.

It is important to cover what the book is *not*. It is not a scientific treatise although scientific and technical approaches are used. It is not a "how-to-do-it" manual although moderate detail on "steps to be taken" is provided in some of the case studies. It is not an attempt to show that the field is either all quantitative or all qualitative; it urges the practitioner to use everything that contributes to client problem-solving.

This type of treatise is not often encountered on the shelves of book-sellers; there may be several reasons for this. One is that the most active practitioners seem to be always bound for the next project; they may feel that there is no time for extra-curricular projects beyond attending professional meetings, giving professional papers or seminars, and attending conferences for CEU points.

Another is that the impulse to write is put off until retirement; then, there are too many other interests that get in the way. A third reason is the perception that others have already covered the topics one way or another. Of course, any given practitioner may simply lack interest in writing a book.

It occurs to the author that there is a need to address the practice of I/O Psychology from an eclectic point of view. This field, like its cousins, clinical and educational psychology, is using scientific methods to increase reliability and validity of measurement. At the same time, it is not possible to cast aside the aesthetic, cultural, and philosophical factors that have influenced these fields from the beginning. Said otherwise, the pursuit of truth in applied psychology seems to venture into the realms of increasing the potential of measurement on the one hand and understanding human behavior on the other.

Given the current expansion of applied psychology, all kinds of studies are taking place from both theoretical and empirical points of view. At the most recent SIOP convention, for example, papers, symposiums, and workshops covered hundreds of topics. It is not possible to review such endeavors in a single book. The organizing principle for this book, therefore, was to present an outline of how various techniques were used to address various client problems. Chapters of the book, then, are arranged around such techniques. Additionally, there are chapters on professional ethics, business ethics, and cultural topics.

As said earlier, the target audiences for the book are new professionals, experienced professionals, and interested human resource professionals. Also, there are points of view in the book that should be of interest to executives and some members of the general reading public. Meanwhile, more specific reasons for why the book was written for professionals are listed below: (The phrase "general practitioner" as used below is defined as someone who is trained and qualified in the various sub-fields of I/O psychology. He/she is not confined in the practice to specialty areas such as training, organizational development, selection, attitude research, etc.)

1) To preserve for others some of the professional experiences of the author and to provide models for client problem-solving.
2) To present a case for the utility of the I/O general practitioner.
3) To demonstrate the variety of assignments a general practitioner could take on.
4) To illustrate problem-solving techniques that may not be taught in graduate school.
5) To comment on the effects of the difference in focus between academicians and practitioners.
6) To comment on how the "art" of practice balances with the "science."
7) To comment on the ethics of the field in a way that addresses the role of the I/O practitioner as well as the behavior.

8) To cover how poor business ethics may contribute to poor psychological practice.

9) To discuss the merits of an independent practice.

10) To present the results of an analysis of the I/O job. This should benefit new professionals who are searching for ideas for self-development and also senior psychologists who will be evaluating the performance of their colleagues and subordinates.

The Gap between Theory and Practice

It is appropriate to bring up the "gap" between theory and practice at this point. The book is written by someone with both teaching and research experience, yet it probably has the practitioner's biases rather than those of the academician. This does not mean, however, that practitioners do not attempt to incorporate as much science as possible within the scope of a given project. At this point I will address my own observations as to the reasons for the gap; most of these address the differences between academicians and practitioners.

First, academics tend to specialize within the field in terms of both research and practice. For example, if a professor is interested in employee selection, he/she is more likely to have clients who need selection programs rather than other disciplines within the field (training, training design, organizational development, survey research, etc.).

Second, practitioners tend to make their income from client fees whereas academics have both institutional salaries *and* client fees. This discrepancy leads to a situation in which academics can make a living without having to rely solely on satisfying client needs and gaining repeat business. Psychologists who work as employees of large organizations are also paid mostly by salary. Often they are discouraged from taking on extra work outside the company or agency.

Third, as they are monitoring research done within the field, reviewers and journal editors search for professionals whose work is on the "cutting edge" of the field. Academicians are more likely to be on the edge because of their concentration in one or two major areas. Practitioners tend to have less time to evaluate critically the various products of research; also, as a group, they tend to lack adequate time to develop a body of research. This is often true of "company" or agency psychologists as well; their organizations demand all of their time as they are creating and implementing programs used for their own purposes rather than for the purposes of the field in general.

Fourth, academicians tend to teach the "science" to their graduate students rather than the "techniques" which can be used to directly address organizational problems. Examples of "techniques" include supervisory and management training, executive coaching, managerial assessment, survey feedback, the design of technical training, selection, promotion, etc. In some cases, the reason for this is that it is not likely for an academician to wish to share a technique with graduate students who could be potential competitors in the future. Also, of course, the academician could feel it to be his/her job to teach underlying theory and that graduate students should develop their own techniques down the road.

Fifth, a professor may write a scientific paper with knowledge itself as a goal along with a statement of how the findings relate to a body of knowledge plus a warning that more research should be done before conclusions can be drawn. This perspective is necessary, of course, but it is of little help to the practitioner. The demand for problem-solving in a client organization is strong and keeps the practitioner busy with program development and the application of existing technology rather than taking on pure research projects. For example, the author is familiar with a program obtained by a university I/O department for work in a prison system. The project was scheduled to be complete in a year, and it actually took three years because of opportunities to elaborate the theory building rather than work directly on actual problems in the prison system.

It is appropriate here to discuss Hersey-Blanchard's Situational Leadership Theory. It is based on a number of approaches and practice techniques including Likert's System I-IV, Fleishman's Structure/Consideration model, Argyris' concept of employee maturity, and Transactional Analysis (Berne). It is very helpful to the field that these two authors have taken the time to construct their own theory of leadership with the assistance of those mentioned above. Their work stands as one example of how practitioners can develop a working theory and follow it in their practice.

Practitioners in both clinical and I/O psychology are justified in addressing real problems even though their techniques could be a bit more developed. The key here is borrowed from clinical psychologists who argue that, if an approach to psychotherapy is theory-based and seems to have obtained some statistical success, then it may be worth using. Examples here would include cognitive therapy, Rogerian therapy, behaviorist approaches, etc.

Philosophy of the Author

It is appropriate for the reader to know something of the background and philosophy of the author at this point. He originally intended to study clinical psychology and did through the master's level. However, given the opportunity to work for a management consulting firm, he took it and did contract work with the USAF Human Resources Laboratory and also market research and manufacturing studies. The practice of this particular firm was to use people both inside and outside of their fields of academic involvement. Next he moved to the HQ location and continued this type of practice while attending graduate school in I/O psychology. After becoming a principal, he founded an I/O firm and most of the cases presented in the book come from this time period. Some of the cases presented were performed in collaboration with other psychologists. Most, however, are individual projects of the author.

Actually, organizational psychology is both a science and an art. It requires the investigative rigor of science and yet one cannot practice it without being aware of the values, morals, ethics, traditions, and philosophies involved in the human condition. Good plays and dramas, for example, reflect the human condition. It is said that a rush to live theater occurred in Germany at the close of World War II because citizens wanted to reflect about who they were, what they had been, and what they might become once the atrocities of Hitler's government had been put behind them. Several movies, plays and novels such as *Platoon, Rollerball, One Flew over the Cuckoo's Nest, The Office, Death of a Salesman,* etc., make powerful psychological points. These will be discussed in a following chapter.

At this point, some preliminary comments about ethics should be made. Often I/O Psychologists, who are for the most part not licensed to practice in their state of residence, do not have a direct reminder of the ethics required in their practices. Many attempt to follow the Ethical Guidelines published by the American Psychological Association, but this author's opinion of their adherence to this code is not really comparable to that followed by clinicians. Rodney Lowman (2006) has edited ethical guidelines for the I/O Psychologist which are fitting for the profession. These reflect the nature of desired practice in the same manner as do the APA Guidelines reflect the desired practice of clinicians.

I/O Psychologists who are not licensed by the state of their residence risk having less knowledge of their duty to protect the public because they are not asked to meet yearly Continuing Educational Unit (CEU) requirements. The book offers both concrete direction and experience that give us pause for thought. Hopefully its critiques of the field will take us where we need to be—thinking holistically, looking for root causes of problems, avoiding the substitution of intellectual skills for disciplined thinking, and focusing on problem-solving as well as theory building.

It is very important that social science not fall into the hands of persons who would manipulate people instead of help them. It was possible for World War II European scientists to convince some of their number that they were merely performing basic research in nuclear physics rather than creating an atomic bomb. It took a smuggled letter from Einstein to convince Niels Bohr that his research, performed in Norway, could facilitate the creation of a bomb which could be used. Bohr immediately arranged secret transport for himself to England. He joined the Allies' war effort, but not before Churchill gave him a lecture about being naïve with respect to the bomb's actual capabilities.

It is the preference of the author that persons destined for the I/O field have adequate orientation in the liberal arts, including such topics as philosophy, literature, and history. Business courses are valuable and understanding the language of business is important, but there is no need to "major in business" to fulfill a preliminary requirement for preparation for I/O psychology. This is the type of book that offers both concrete directions and that give one pause for thought. Hopefully its point of view will take us closer to where we need to be.

More Preliminary Thoughts

This book should be of value because it describes consulting experiences that may be of benefit to other practitioners, be they new to the field (apprentice level) or already experienced (journeyman level). This is not because of their superiority but because they may suggest a different way of doing things.

Secondly, the book could be of value because of its rarity. It is a fair statement that most consultants are preoccupied with the "next" project and may not have or take time to reflect and put together a history of their experiences as organizational builders.

Third, the author develops and presents his philosophy of consulting in an integrated manner. There are, of course, those who would argue that philosophy is not as important as a correct use of applied science and technology. The author will sometimes differ with such a point of view and explain his reasons for doing so.

Fourth, it is important to the author that techniques developed by him not be lost to the next generation. It may be that such techniques will continue to be valuable as time marches onward. We will, however, leave it to future practitioners to decide if ideas created for the present will shed light on problems faced by organizations in the future.

1. INTRODUCTION

The Client/Consultant Interface

It seems likely that all professionals, regardless of their field of endeavor, will mature in technical prowess, general insight, and ability to influence the client as well as their colleagues. Different professions do not seem to mature at the same pace, however. Accountants, for example, are taught to tackle major tasks soon after receiving a BBA degree. Attorneys reach a certain maturation level within two or three years after receiving a J.D. degree. Physicians undergo a maturation process in a formal, step-wise manner by undergoing an externship, an internship, and a hospital residency.

I/O Psychologists typically undergo one or two externships, receive a PhD or PsyD in the field and then receive fulltime or Post-Doc positions. There is no absolute standard for the I/O field. Some actually find work at the Bachelor's level although it is usually a narrow application of an approach created by a PhD; the application is usually one emphasizing organizational change, test administration, or perhaps applying a structured interview. As mentioned earlier, the bachelor's level person usually applies a memorized approach and is basically without much knowledge of the theory or theories behind the approach. At the master's level, there are professionals who can learn several applications.

The PhD or PsyD degree is required for comprehension of the basis for holistic or true problem-solving. Job experience is also a "must" for persons who would take on projects in all of the major applications

Too often a managing professional within a midsize to large consulting firm will "sell" a project, get it underway, and then leave it in the hands of one senior and several junior consultants. The main problem here is that, with the managing professional moving on to acquire or service other clients, those left with the task of project execution may encounter "mid-stream" difficulties which they have little experience in handling. This situation can be ameliorated by increasing the participation of the manager. Too often, however, the overhead needs of the business require that person to be elsewhere. A smaller firm with less overhead may be able to dedicate the manager to the project. Also, it may be able to dedicate a general practitioner to the project because it will not have to acquire specialists. In addition, the general practitioner may be able to bill his/her time at less cost to the client.

This is only one argument for the general practitioner model. Another very important argument is that the focus of the I/O can change during the mid-stream portion of the engagement. An appropriate analogy can be taken from the medical profession. Say, for example, that a hepatologist (liver doctor) had been treating a patient for cirrhosis. The next set of blood lab tests showed, however, that a tumor-marker enzyme was high whereas it had not been in a previous blood test. The physician may now have to apply a cancer treatment which would address a different problem than cirrhosis. He may be able to do this if he is trained both in liver function and cancer of the GI system and has a broader perspective.

Examples of the Need for Multiple Skills in a Practitioner

The I/O field is full of such complexities and new data that require interpretation. A few examples will be mentioned below although they will be addressed in more detail in a chapter to follow. The first example is from a plant in which 20 members of the maintenance organization were interviewed in the performance of a job analysis of the maintenance supervisory position. Halfway through the process, it became apparent to the author that many of the interviewees were offering more information about their work attitudes and organizational dynamics at the company than about the supervisory job as such. The author completed the interviews but wrote two reports instead of one. The first was the job analysis itself, which listed major duties and tasks performed by incumbents and provided recommendations for pre-supervisory promotion measures. The second report, written confidentially for plant management, provided an analysis of concerns and attitudes concerning the maintenance organization. It had become apparent to the consultant that concerns of incumbents should be addressed before any new programs could be installed; otherwise, new procedures or techniques might not be successful in implementation. Permission was obtained from the interviewees to report on both attitudes as well as job requirements.

In a second example of the value of preserving the general practitioner role, a tendency of some specialized professionals should be discussed. For example, the author was in conversation with an I/O psychologist who did a large proportion of his work in management development seminars. He asked the author whether he did management training, he was told "yes." Before another word could be said, the psychologist said, "What instrument do you use?" At this point neither of us had discussed the various forms of management development. The author was being presented with the idea that training plus feedback from a particular instrument was all that was needed to improve managerial performance. The validity of this instrument was not discussed. The person was offering the same seminar to managerial groups regardless of their previous orientation, the company culture, or the particular types of individuals involved. There was no consideration of other measures or approaches; a group of field managers would get the same training as a group of executives. No consideration of individual differences was considered; the assumption was made that the particular theory being taught was the only theory.

A third example is from an assessment psychologist who uses the same computerized assessment no matter who the client is or what the job is. He expresses pride of ownership of this technique, which is inexpensive to administer and not difficult to interpret. When the author was approached by this person (his boss) to use the technique for the selection of over-the-road truck drivers, the boss was told that a literature search and a job analysis had already been done indicating that the best way to predict tenure in this case was with biodata. The point here is that someone who is committed to an assessment procedure is often likely to utilize that procedure out of pride of ownership and possible financial gain. The mission is to select tool(s) that are appropriate for the job. The proper process here, of course, is to study the situation (job), to choose an experimental test or set of items that is likely to be valid in the situation and to disregard any temptation to put the test ahead of the problem.

The remaining chapters of the book will highlight cases presented to the psychologist during his career. These occur on a more or less random basis, depending on the client's situation at the time. We will voyage through the territories of selection, promotion, training, performance appraisal, market research, vocational psychology, organizational analysis and development, business ethics, psychologist ethics, and aesthetics.

2. First Major Case Study
(Selection on the Basis of Values)

It is appropriate at this point to enter into our first major case study. The reader will remember that the book is organized around cases instead of classical topical areas. We are going to begin with a personnel issue that is occurring in school districts across the country, i.e., the selection of football coaches. This one turned out to be "selection on the basis of values." The case was not a client assignment; rather it had a different etiology. The son of the author was a high school baseball and football coach; the father (the author) heard many stories about football, how it was played in high school, the types of head coaches, etc. It seemed to this writer, who had played high school football, that a coach selection device could be constructed and used in the "field," so to speak. The process used by school boards and superintendents seemed subjective. Often they would look for a "winner" to be head coach but just as often they would look for a mature manager or someone who would be very concerned about the players and their academic and athletic development. It occurred to the author that each school board could have its own set of values that could be objectified in some manner so that they could be matched with the values of the candidates for a vacant position. The motive for the author here was to construct a good instrument or process that could be of use to school districts.

As the idea began to develop and work went forward, it became apparent that several decisions had to be made. One would have to determine what type of job analysis to use, what type of instrument or process could be successful, how to determine a method for criterion construction, how to construct the instrument/process, and how to compare a predictor score with a criterion score. A number of school districts would have to be contacted so that both specificity and generalizability could be approached. Also, an inexpensive project was called for because there was no budget for the study other than the author's personal resources. In addition, a target audience for job analytic interviews had to be established. School board members were not really subject matter experts because their knowledge of the game was primarily that of a spectator. Also, they were not close enough to the locker room to have adequate knowledge of the non-game aspects of the sport (coaching strategy, administrative aspects, how coaches treated the players in practice, etc.). Coaches themselves were so ingrained in their own approaches that they would find it difficult to find merit in the style or values of someone else.

There was another population who did have a systematic knowledge of the game and the characteristics of coaches. This would be athletic directors (A.D.'s) who had an overview of the game and of the kinds of coaches who have failed and succeeded in the past. They were more likely to have a holistic view of the game and a personal view from their own experience as coaches. It was decided, then, to interview at least 20 A.D.'s from as many school districts. The interview was designed to be general in nature; the A.D.'s were asked to talk in a narrative fashion about the traits/factors which characterize a good coach. The interviews were conducted by the author in two metropolitan areas. Typical questions asked were as follows:

- What were the qualities of a good coach?
- What were typical differences between a good and bad coach?
- What were the areas of competency found in a high performing coach?
- What are typical skills/abilities found in a high performing coach?

After the author and a staff consultant read and re-read the interview results, the answers tended to cluster in the general areas of work values. Typical answers included

- Caring about the kids.
- Being driven to win.
- Not showing a temper during a game.
- Being a good administrator.

Analysis of the material produced by the A.D.'s showed that there were seven clusters, all of which were categories of values that would be held by coaches or coaching candidates. Now the researcher must develop an instrument that would measure a candidate's values on the one hand and the school board's preference for particular values on the other. For example, if a candidate held highly to a "win at any cost" value, for there to be a match, the average school board would have to rate that particular value as very desirable. Both must be measured in terms of the seven trait clusters (values) to enable a matching of the school board's overall consensus with the score of any given candidate.

First, the values themselves. Exhibit 1 shows some detail of description of each without any being in a particular order. The author assumes here that measurement of values could be as good a predictor as, say, personality, work habits, cognitive abilities, etc.

At this point the reader should have more detail on how the candidates' profile of values was measured and how the school board's consensus was measured. A precedent for measuring the candidate's profile has been set by Gordon's "Personal and Interpersonal Survey of Values" (2006). Here, after the number of values has been determined, the item arrangement is organized so that the test compares the candidate's preference for each with his preference for every other value covered by the test. An example item is listed below in the language of a coaching application:

Most Liked	Most Disliked	
■	❏	Keeping kids' morale up
❏	■	Keeping records straight
❏	❏	Holding one's temper
❏	❏	Winning

This person's item score gives her/him +1 on "Concern for Kids," -1 for "Administrative Management, "0" for "Personal Maturity," and "0" for "Personal Ambition/Desire to Win." For the entire questionnaire, 35 items of this nature are required. The possible range for any scale is from -35 to +35 points.

With respect to the measurement of school board values, a group exercise in which all seven values were ranked by consensus was conducted. (These became the dimensions on the values rating measures.) Tables 1 and 2 show how the match takes place between ranks for two different candidates. The first has a total score of 12, which is relatively high; the second has a total score of 18.

Exhibit
Specific Values Held by Coaches as Inferred from A.D.'s

1. Personal Ambition/Desire to Win: This involves one's belief in the value of having a winning record; having personal ambition.
2. Personal Maturity: This involves one's belief in the value of self-control, avoiding negative emotional displays, and making good decisions while under stress.
3. Concern for the Kids: This involves one's interests in the development and well-being of the students participating in athletics.
4. Communications and Public Relations: This involves one's concern for listening and talking to and just being in touch with the public.
5. Managing and Motivating: This involves one's concern for motivating, supervising, and delegating properly to both students and staff.
6. Administrative Motivation: This involves one's concern for planning, organizing, and performing the administrative aspects of the job.
7. Integrating the Athletic Program with other District Priorities: This involves respect for the school district organization and balancing the needs of the athletic program with those of the other departments.

Table 1
Difference in Score between School Board Consensus and First Individual Candidate's Score (1 = high score; 7 = low)

Value	Ranking by Board	Ranking by Candidate	Difference
Personal ambition/Win	1	2	1
Personal maturity	3	5	2
Concern for kids	2	3	1
Communication/PR	7	4	3
Managing and Motivating	4	6	2
Administrative Motivation	5	7	2
Integrating Athletic with other departments	6	5	1
Total Difference (Absolute value)			12

Table 2

Difference in Score between School Board Consensus and Second Individual Candidate's Score (1 = high score; 7 = low)

Value	Ranking by Board	Ranking by Candidate	Difference
Personal ambition/Win	1	5	4
Personal maturity	3	3	0
Concern for kids	2	7	5
Communication/PR	7	2	5
Managing and Motivating	4	1	3
Administrative Motivation	5	4	1
Integrating Athletic with other departments	6	6	0
Total Difference (Absolute value)			18

It will be, of course, easier to distinguish between candidates when enough total scores have been accumulated to enable the creation of norms. Meanwhile, the candidate with a score of 12 seems to be preferable to the one with a score of 18. That is to say that the first candidate's value profile matches the consensus of the school board better than the second candidate.

In summary, then, this method of selection requires

(1) An in-depth type of interview with true experts in the field;
(2) A listing of values required in the job;
(3) A technique for measuring the values of candidates;
(4) A technique for reaching consensus among members of the controlling board or committee as to the relative order of the values;
(5) A technique for matching the values of the candidates with those of the board.

This selection technique probably works best with managers or professionals whose functions are somewhat known to the public. This could include police or fire captains, coaches, school principals, other types of civil servants, etc.

Content validity is accomplished by derivation of factors from true experts in a given field. Follow-up validation is certainly possible with the "difference" scores.

3. A PROJECT REQUIRING MULTIPLE APPROACHES

The previous case description focused on "selection" as a strategy. Pieces of a selection approach were put together for the construction of a final, single strategy. In this next case, what appeared to be a selection problem actually was much broader and, before the study reached a conclusion, techniques of selection research, training needs analysis, employee retention, survey feedback, and root-cause analysis were all utilized. It would have been difficult for a specialist in just one of these areas to visualize the overall pattern although there turned out to be plenty here for a selection point of view, a training point of view, an attitude research approach, and a survey feedback approach.

The client was a large, over-the-road trucking company with approximately 1400 owner-operators, each the owner of a truck with an overnight cab (a tractor) that pulls a company-owned trailer. The standard recruiting and driver development sequence was as follows:

1) Advertisements in large city newspapers offering a low down payment and monthly payment to acquire one of these tractors capable of pulling loads across the entire country.

2) An unstructured telephone interview.

3) Two weeks of training, the first focusing on required driver records, miscellaneous paperwork, FTC and other legal requirements; the second week was behind-the-wheel activities, learning how to operate the cab—including making turns, backing up the trailer, performing simple maintenance. All of the second week was confined to a large yard dedicated to the training function.

4) The purchase of the tractor was financed by the company. They were either new or used; the used ones were often picked up by the company after someone resigned from the business or had gone bankrupt

on the road. The initial maintenance condition of the used tractors was not normally guaranteed by the company.

5) Acquainting oneself with the driver accounting, dispatch, planning, counseling, and general operations functions of the company.

6) Starting the process of receiving loads (assignments) from a dispatcher.

The consulting project was requested by the company and the consultant was aware of the results of a previous study done with line-haul revenue as a criterion; now, however, driver tenure (turnover) was the problem. The actual turnover rate was approximately 100% annually (as computed by the HR Department), meaning that ½ of the drivers in a single year left the fleet. The industry average, again provided by the HR Department was about 50% per year. The 100% figure was too high for the company to tolerate. Fortunately, tests, measures, and biodata questions had been administered 2-3 years earlier at the hiring stage of the previous project. This gave the project a head start, since tenure data was available on all of these individuals (161 in number). These individuals were divided into three groups as follows:

1) Stayed with the company up to two months and then resigned or were terminated (N = 52).

2) Stayed for 3-8 months and then resigned or were terminated (N = 52).

3) Stayed for 9-24 months and were still with the fleet (N = 57).

Data were taken from measures of work interests, biodata, and a cognitive scale. Table 3 shows the results from the item, "population of childhood residence." It is clear that being reared in a small town enhances tenure at the company. Table 4 shows the relationship between previous driver experience and tenure. It seems that having been a driver before is also a positive tenure element.

Other variables (statistics not shown here) also predict driver tenure, including distance of present residence from a city of more than size 500,000, family health, interest in outdoor activities, wanting to get into the business because of the opportunity rather than because it was "just a job" or to "see the sights" across the country, etc. All of these and other variables differentiated significantly among the various tenure groups. However, when the variables were weighted and put together as a scale, the resulting distribution in a cross-validation sample shed a new light on the problem. To increase tenure over the base rate of 6 months, 80% of applicants would have to be rejected. The company was unwilling to live with this level of rejection for a small increase in tenure on the grounds of cost and difficulty of recruitment. To be aligned with the results, for example, they would have to switch their advertising to small town newspapers and the cost/inquiry would be substantially increased. Given that the company was still interested in the project and that the consultant had begun to pick up stories about the treatment of the drivers, it was decided to perform an employee attitude survey with a survey feedback process built in.

Table 3
Relationship between Population Residence and Tenure of Operator

Population of Childhood Residence	Short Tenured Operators	Medium Tenured Operators	Long Tenured Operators
Rural, less than 2000	7 (13%)	9 (18%)	20 (35%)
2001-100,000	25 (48%)	32 (61%)	27 (18%)
100,001 or more	20 (39%)	11 (21%)	10 (18%)
Total	52 (100%)	52 (100%)	57 (100%)

Chi square = 13.09
Significance level = .025 for 4 df

Table 4
Previous Driver Experience versus Tenure as an Operator

Been Trucker Before	Short Tenured Operators	Medium Tenured Operators	Long Tenured Operators
Yes	13 (25%)	15 (29%)	28 (49%)
No	39 (75%)	37 (71%)	29 (51%)
Total	52 (100%)	52 (100%)	57 (100%)

Chi square = 8.17
Significance level = .02 with 2 df

Telephone interviews with drivers inquired as to driver treatment, specific problems with the departments serving the drivers, why drivers were leaving, communications, adequacy of training, the quality of tractors, etc. Groups of questions were then constructed with each of the company sections in mind and why people would leave or did leave. About 1200 questionnaires were mailed to present drivers and 600 to terminated drivers. Returns were about 600 from current drivers and 300 from terminated drivers. Some of the questions were open-ended and differences in the written responses from present and terminated drivers were extracted.

Results are summarized below in narrative form:

Driver Training: Training was adequate for paperwork and reports including the Federal Transportation Commission (FTC) component. Road and city training was not adequate. Training in the "lot" was performed but making deliveries in cities was not covered. Information about operating efficiently was not covered nor were points like what it costs in fuel to run the heater in the cab during a cold night. Information about alternate routes was not covered. Information about cost and availability of maintenance was not covered.

Route Planning: Planners were fair at arranging for drivers to be present and available at customer sites but they were poor at estimating destination times plus how long it would take to load and unload a trailer. Keeping track of "dead-headed" tractors was poor. In a notable case, a tractor deadheaded from San Francisco to Los Angeles met another one at a truck stop halfway between the cities. It was deadheaded to San Francisco, and the drivers met (by chance) and discovered that both of their vehicles were being sent to the other's point of origin (a misuse). Both were angry that they were asked to spend this wasted mileage when each could have taken the other's load in a swap.

Dispatch: The drivers were not getting loads at expected intervals because of poor planning, mis-assigned loading, and some corruption among the ranks (drivers having to bribe certain dispatchers for loads).

Driver Counseling: If a driver was struggling, counselors at HQ were supposed to assist the drivers with their financial problems, not getting home often enough, getting maintenance on the road, completing insurance claims, etc. In reality, the counselors were frustrated with the drivers and ended up disciplining them more than facilitating their success.

Tractor Sales: The people in charge of selling tractors to the new recruits were passing on used equipment without major repair and making a profit for their department on these sales. Perhaps this department was the worst in terms of not facilitating driver success because working equipment is necessary for the driver to make a living.

Driver Accounting: Like Driver Counseling, this department was punishing the drivers; in this case it was by being a poor administrator of the process of delivering driver payments. Also it had increased the activity of administering fines and pursuing other financial punishments.

In accordance with survey feedback technique (French, 1988) each department was given its own specific feedback on the survey. Department managers and staff were asked to respond with plans for increasing retention and with plans for responding to the feedback before it was passed upward to top management. This did happen and the responses were constructive and realistic. Over a year or so, however, retention in the fleet had not improved.

The consultant, dissatisfied that neither selection nor retention strategies were working to cut turnover, sought other solutions. He and his staff interviewed a number of middle and senior managers. Topics discussed included the business in general, differences between an owner-operator and a salaried fleet, plus why the owner-operators were treated badly. Overall, this company had become a "house divided against itself." Training was not really training, tractor sales was making an internal profit on its "product," operations was providing poor planning, inadequate dispatching, no counseling, and poor financial assistance. No one seemed to be able to explain why these situations existed. Then a discussion among managers revealed that the Sales Department (so far not studied) was functionally in charge of fleet size. At first, this fact does not appear to be threatening. The logic would be that "sales" is making commitments to customers and should be the ones who stock up on the equipment needed to move customer products.

There was a basic problem here, however. Sales was not in sync with Operations on tractor or trailer supply, and it looked like they had not intended to be. The sales department was making fleet size decisions without consulting Operations. To leave out Operations would be to bring in tractors and trailers without knowledge of road conditions, maintenance problems, morale, whether orders had been completed or not, etc. In the final analysis, Operations, in spite of its mistakes, was in daily contact with drivers and are the best determiners of fleet size. The president of the company, however, had come up the sales ladder and wanted to be in command of things related to sales and marketing. He was also caught up in the contest of having the best sales record the company had ever shown.

Finally, there was an explanation for the turnover, which key individuals had apparently ignored or pretended didn't exist. Given the turnover caused by the fact that Operations couldn't keep up with the flow of new equipment, each of the departments had gone into a cover-up position in which they felt that they couldn't be held liable. In fact, all of them were liable as long as sales was dominant. It was necessary for fleet size decisions to go back to Operations where Sales would state its requirements and Operations would size the fleet properly instead of optimistically.

The recommendation was given to the company that fleet size decisions be returned to Operations, but it didn't change at first—possibly because of the "ego" of the president. Turnover remained around 100% for at least a year. Then it began to drop slowly to 50% and down to 37% two years later with the installment of the selection strategy (with a lower cut score), a retention strategy involving mostly driver treatment, and with the change of fleet size determination now highly influenced by Operations.

This was a complex study that took a considerable amount of investigation to come up with a "root cause" of the problem. It was very important that multiple paths were used; if the primary investigator had used only selection or retention as possible paths, a holistic solution might not have been reached. Again, the need for a consultant who had command of a number of approaches was an absolute requirement for the intervention to be successful.

4. SEVEN TYPES OF JOB ANALYSIS

Job analysis is usually needed on any kind of I/O project. It is absolutely necessary, of course, on selection, promotion, training, or performance evaluation projects. It is beneficial to the reader, at this point, to cover purposes, types, and expected outcomes of various job analysis techniques. A project done without job analysis is likely to "miss the mark" and point in the wrong direction than that required by the assignment.

The Narrative Approach
The first type is the "narrative" approach, in which a few incumbents and some supervisors are interviewed for a picture of the basic responsibilities of the job. Notes are taken by the consultant (an experienced I/O psychologist) and questions such as the following are posed to the job experts mentioned above:

- What are the 5 or 6 basic responsibilities of the job?
- What is the most time-consuming part of the job?
- How long does it take to learn this job?
- What is the most critical part of the job?
- How much training does it take to perform this job?

These questions seem simple, but most respondents will answer them at length in a detailed fashion. After the interviewer consolidates his/her notes and also consults publicized documentaries on the job (such as departmental job descriptions, manuals, regulations, etc.), a paragraph form narrative is written which contains statements about the tasks to be mastered and the skills, knowledge, and abilities (KSAs) needed to perform the job. This type of analysis is used mostly to update job descriptions, to provide job content for content validation studies, and to acquaint managers with the job itself.

The Work Diary Approach

The second type of job analysis is the work diary approach. Each incumbent is given a five-day notebook in which daily activities are written and some kind of "time spent" percentage for each major activity is estimated by the incumbent. After 5-10 incumbents have completed their notebooks, the job analyst summarizes time spent across categories and comes up with a picture of how the various activities are distributed over a week's time. This technique offers an overview of the job in the language of the incumbent; it is good for projects which require two types of job analysis, this one offering a check on the other.

The Direct Observation Approach

Direct observation is the third type of job analysis to be discussed in this book. It involves the analyst's presence on the job to actually "see and hear" things being done. The observer is free to ask occasional questions as long as he/she doesn't interfere with tasks being accomplished. This type works to supplement training needs analyses and for determining activity levels in the workforce. For example, in a job justification study, it helps a great deal to know whether individuals are actually "busy" or not. The way in which tasks are being done can be observed as well. For example, an observer, while studying the night shift at a police department, noticed that an incumbent police officer was taking flash pictures of a crime scene without checking to see whether there was adequate light to highlight details in pictures generated.

The Task Analysis Approach

The fourth method to be discussed here is "task analysis." It is a major form of job analysis and takes more professional and incumbent labor than the others previously discussed. Preliminary research and interviews are used to find the major "parts" and "duties" of the job and each, with the help of Subject Matter Experts (SMEs), is broken down into task statements with action verbs and direct objects in each sentence.

With respect to the USAF method (Christal, 1988) of task analysis, the statements are rated by incumbent samples on such scales as "time spent," "difficulty," and "criticality." When used in military settings, the computer analysis (called CODAP for Computerized Occupational Data Analysis Program), clusters incumbents into job types. The results are used to determine career "shred-outs," from which new jobs can be generated. For example, the photo intelligence career field is now split into people who monitor intelligence photography and those who interpret pictures obtained. Also, the results are used to provide input to specialists who write career development and promotional tests within career ladders. Test authors can determine which are the most time-consuming, difficult, and critical tasks in a career field and they can create and weight test items according to these parameters.

The author is familiar with the use of a CODAP analysis on a very large police department. It was very useful in determining task overlap among the various subspecialties in a police department so that specific training and promotional ladders could be developed. For example, there is a patrolman, an auto accident patrolman, an investigative patrolman, a detective, a jailer, a community police officer, other subspecialties, and of course sergeants, lieutenants, captains, assistant chiefs, etc. By using the results of heavy preliminary interviewing and creating a multitude of task statements, the entire police force was covered with one lengthy task analysis questionnaire to be rated by incumbents.

The Critical Incident Approach

The fifth method is the critical incident technique (Flanagan). This method involves the collection of job behavior incidents from both incumbents and supervisors. In an interview, the job analyst asks these personnel to describe three incidents of very effective job behavior and three of very ineffective behavior they have observed in job holders. For each story, the analyst asks what led up to it, what actually happened, and what the consequences were. After a large number of such stories have been collected (i.e., 200-300), independent judges classify the themes in these stories into behavioral or performance dimensions. For most jobs, 10-20 behavioral dimensions or categories can be determined. Some of these will be illustrated in following chapters. Results can be used to construct performance dimensions for test selection and validation, performance evaluation, the design of training programs, and the documentation of KSAs as they develop and change over time.

The quantity of behavioral incidents can also be used to weight the importance of behaviors in a job. For example, if 20% of the stories emphasize two-way communication and interpersonal skills, then a good argument is being made for this factor to be present in selection, promotion, training, etc.

Later in the book a case will be made for weighting the elements in a performance document based on the number or volume of critical incident themes collected from the research.

The Work Sampling Approach

The sixth to be mentioned here represents a class of job studies that originated within the field of industrial engineering. Others would be time-and-motion study, workflow planning, job design, etc. Time-and-motion study is an attempt to determine how many "person-minutes" go into the steps of a manufacturing line. Also it is used for how many person-hours are involved in completing a lengthy manufacturing process. It is basic to the process of manufacturing line improvement.

"Work sampling" (Sheth, 2000) is a random sampling process that is composed of visual snapshots of behavior that has been categorized on a predetermined basis; categories might include "work," "idle," "getting supplies," "personal," and "in transit." It is useful, like "direct observation," in determining the activity or "work" percent of the job shown by the average incumbent. According to custom and practicality, an average of 70% would show a high level of work activity whereas a figure of 30% would show a low level. In the next chapter, the book offers a detailed example of the results of a "work sampling" project.

The Position Analysis Questionnaire

The seventh technique is one based on "job elements," as is found in the Position Analysis Questionnaire, or PAQ (Jeanneret, 1971). This technique involves job elements that apply to all non-management jobs and are descriptive of elements of the world of work in general. It can be used to determine the attributes of most jobs; results can be used in synthetic validation, job evaluation, compensation and other types of projects. The PAQ is based on the theory that there is a finite number of job elements in the human workplace and that trained raters can use the PAQ to perform a complete analysis on any job. A second instrument is used on managerial jobs (The Managerial PAQ).

There are other types of job analysis, but we will curtail our discussion at this point because our purpose in this chapter was to provide the reader with an overview prior to discussion of cases which will appear in following chapters.

5. Work Sampling Project

We will now continue the case studies promised in the Prologue. This one involving work sampling is presented because the nature of the study changed in mid-stream. This turns out to be a reason for using a general practitioner instead of a specialist on the project. To begin, the manager of a medium-sized chemical plant called the author to discuss the productivity of the hourly maintenance workforce. After a meeting with the client at the plant, it became apparent that he wanted a quantitative study to be performed in which productive and non-productive behaviors could be identified and measured. Although he was an engineer by training, he seemed to be acquainted with methods for studying the activity of the workforce. His preference was for the "work sampling" technique, in which random "glimpses" of worker behavior could be taken on a periodic, daily basis. The consultant was told that there was a productivity problem in the delivery of maintenance services such as pump repair, gearbox disassembly and assembly, and shop activities such as the operation of a drill press or a lathe.

The consultant discussed various methods that could be used to study productivity, but agreed with the client that work sampling would have the advantage of being a direct and reliable measure of both productive and non-productive work behaviors. This technique would be used if the workers gave their permission to be observed and the sampling of the behaviors was extensive.

A plan was devised whereby each worker was sampled once per day for a period of 30 consecutive work days. Such a procedure guaranteed that at least 1200 observations would be made, that being the number required for + 3% accuracy at the 95% confidence level. One sampling per day seemed to offer minimal disruption in the work of the maintenance supervisors. Each was contacted by a secretary once per day at a time determined by a random number generator. Also, each supervisor observed his own behavior by recording in narrative form a brief description of what he/she was doing at the time contacted by the secretary. At this time, they walked through the workplace and sampled all of the craft persons assigned to them—usually about six people.

The supervisors, of course, had to be trained to use the method and this was done by the consultant during a four-hour session. Course content consisted of the basics of work measurement/sampling, practice work sampling exercises, and open discussion through which pertinent activity categories were developed. The following categories were determined for classifying the work behavior of the maintenance hourly group.

CATEGORY	*EXAMPLES*
(1) Work	- Corrective maintenance
	- Preventive maintenance
	- Safety (putting up scaffolds, getting ropes, etc.)
	- Clean-up
	- Standing watch over a vessel
(2) Vehicular travel	- Travelling in a motorized vehicle or on a bicycle
(3) Foot travel	- Walking to a destination
(4) Storeroom	- At storeroom window
(5) Idle	- Non-productive; waiting
(6) Personal	- Coffee, cigarette, restrooms, etc.

In addition, simple ground rules were developed for project administrative decisions.

Results

Based on 1534 observations during 30 work days, worker activity was distributed as follows:

ACTIVITY CATEGORY	*% TIME*
Work	43.7%
Vehicular travel	7.8%
Foot travel	11.9%
Storeroom	1.5%

Idle	25.6%
Personal	9.5%
Total	100.0%

These figures were stable over a weekly and also on a time-of-day basis. Seven categories of supervisory activity were developed by content-analysis of the supervisors' written descriptions of their own behavior when notified to take a worker sample. Category descriptions and their "scores" in terms of supervisory time spent are presented below:

CATEGORY	% TIME SPENT
(1) Direct supervision: in contact with workers, inspecting their work, discussing the job on site, assigning work	24.0%
(2) Office and paperwork: Performing miscellaneous office tasks, making out schedules, time sheets, purchase orders, writing letters, etc.	28.7%
(3) Consultation: conferring with another supervisor, a manager, a vendor, etc.	28.7%
(4) Meetings	5.3%
(5) Personal, idle, etc.	4.0%
(6) Travel	6.4%
(7) Misc.	2.9%
	100.0%

Given the results above, the question became one of interpretation. Most managers, understanding the need for transit and personal time, would still hope for at least 60% "work" time from the labor force. In the study above, there was only 44% actual work and 26% idle time. The plant manager's hypothesis, that the maintenance force was "slacking off," seemed to be confirmed. This finding was accompanied by the fact that supervisors were not performing enough direct supervision, given that there is an informal industry standard that, to be effective, a supervisor should spend about half of his/her time in direct supervision. The question then became one of "Are the supervisors also slacking off, or is there another reason for their behavior?"

The next step was not called for in the original project design but became necessary as part of a "root cause analysis." The supervisors were shown the results and interviewed by the author. During these interviews, reactions from the work force were brought up. In other words, supervisors had heard from the hourly leaders that the workers might protest if too heavily supervised, and it was implied that this protest could take the form of even lower productivity and more grievances. The supervisors seemed ready to admit that low direct supervision was contributing to the low worker productivity. However, the supervisors also stated that management was reluctant to back up disciplinary actions taken by them. The causative thinking here needed to go beyond a simplistic view. A broader point of view would be as follows:

1) Supervisors were initially behaving as they should, doing their jobs and disciplining when necessary.
2) Workers began complaining about "too much supervision"; the number of grievances went up, and management, fearing lower productivity, began to contradict themselves. On the one hand they needed greater productivity, but on the other hand they would drop hints to supervision that too much discipline is a bad thing.
3) Supervisors, without being told to do so, began to pull back on "direct supervision." Complaints from workers went down until the cycle of events happened again, resulting in decreased productivity.

The author suggested for managers and supervisors to explore and listen to the difficulties of both. Hopefully, a vigorous discussion would soon involve lead workers and then conflict resolution techniques could be brought to bear. The study now was in the province of conflict resolution rather than work measurement and "proving" worker inactivity. The author, then a junior consultant, was pulled off the project because of consultant labor needed at other projects in his firm. He did not see the end of the story with this client; he did recommend that another consulting psychologist pick up and carry it forward.

6. Applications of the Critical Incident Technique

Normally the critical incident technique is used to establish key behavioral dimensions for a given job or a group of jobs. Also, it can provide anchors for performance rating scales. Another use is the formation of behavioral dimensions plus the weighting of these dimensions on the basis of the number of incidents collected in a given study. The reader has been introduced to this technique in a previous chapter.

We will now take on some jobs including technical manager, secondary school teacher, attorney, and programmer/systems analyst. A reason for choosing a sample of professions is to involve the critical incident method with higher level jobs. The incidents gathered in this process are not necessarily physical acts but include mental acts which can be classified as professional performance dimensions. The lists of behavioral dimensions are "content valid" because they are derived totally from the job itself. Each dimension is given a percentage based on the total number of incidents in each divided by the grand total of incidents for a particular job. The totals for all dimensions in a single job, then, would be 100%. Interviewers were undergraduates taking a course in I/O Psychology; these were night classes and most of these students were 25-plus years of age and were employed during the day. The studies were done as class projects in which the students were trained in the method and then made appointments for interviews with people in the fields being studied. The fields were programming, technical management, law (attorneys), and secondary education (high school teachers).

PROGRAMMER: We shall begin with the computer programmer/analyst job. Judging from employment advertisements, one would think that experience with particular programming languages or systems are the key qualifications for hiring. Based on conversations with programmers and analysts, however, one hears that languages can be learned on the job and that other skills/traits may be more important for the hiring process. Exhibit 2 shows the weights given key behavioral dimensions in the job family, including programmer, programmer/analyst, systems analyst and systems manager/supervisor. The reader will notice that work habits

Exhibit 2
Weights of Performance Categories within the
Programming Job Family

Behavioral Category	Programmer	Program-mer/Analyst	Systems Analyst	Systems Supervisor
Work Habits	52%	52%	28%	12%
Interpersonal Skills	28%	28%	32%	48%
Thinking & Analysis	20%	20%	40%	40%

(Initiative, conscientiousness, taking responsibility, and endurance) plus interpersonal skills take on more weight than do those skills relating to thinking and analysis on an overall basis. Work habits take on more weight for the programmer and programmer/analyst job subcategories. The systems analyst needs to know programs and systems whereas the supervisor has a heavy requirement for interpersonal skills. It is one thing to write or install systems but quite another to relate well to clients and fellow workers. The person who can avoid technical jargon will be more successful in client communications. A person may be able to write programs well but forget to document them. He/she may assume there will be no "bugs" in a system that is going to be installed on a Monday and not be available for "debugging" on that day. The data above can be used to direct a selection or promotion program for this field in which much more than just programming knowledge should be assessed.

TECHNICAL MANAGERS: Exhibit 3 presents the summarized key behaviors required in the job of technical manager. The sample for this group of managers included maintenance managers, operations managers, laboratory managers, space science managers, systems managers, hardware manufacturing managers, software development managers, etc. Where possible, managers of managers were interviewed; otherwise experienced technical managers were used. It was important to study technical rather than ordinary managers to determine whether a special set of skills was required.

First, task analysis was used to determine how a "time spent" distribution of work performed would look. A set of managers from an appropriate client was used for this. Exhibit 3 shows that "conceptual," "technical," and "human" tasks were performed on roughly an even basis. At business schools, the conventional wisdom is that this classification is "about right." It seems to make sense because it is not difficult to imagine a given manager confronting challenges on each area on a distributed basis.

It turns out, however, that task analysis and critical incident analysis may yield very different results. Exhibit 4 shows that technical and conceptual skills are highly overshadowed by human skills in the execution of the technical manager job. Although this managerial type must show technical and conceptual capacities, if they lack the capabilities for personnel decision-making, training, communications, participative management, coaching, disciplining, maintaining emotional maturity (the "human" skills), they will surely not advance and may fail as a manager. Some people are placed into managerial jobs on the basis of technical and conceptual skills alone; most of us are aware of these personnel and, given the opportunity, will attempt to train, coach, and counsel them. Exhibit 5 shows two such studies performed at different companies; the reader will notice the similarity between the two and perhaps realize that this managerial profile cuts across companies. It is also a type of validation of managerial assessments, which are known to assess most of the factors in the "human" category as well as the "conceptual."

ATTORNEYS: The author was able to schedule interviews with 100 attorneys and paralegals. Interviewers were students in two I/O Psychology undergraduate classes. Groups of the students also developed behavioral dimensions by re-classifying (re-translating; Smith and Kendall) the stories into the categories (performance categories). Exhibit 6 presents a summarized version of the outcome. Attorney subgroupings were (1) assistant district attorneys (ADAs), (2) civil litigators, (3) civil non-litigators, and (4) paralegals (who are not attorneys). Discussion of these four types is needed. The first column shows that work habits and organization is the most heavily weighted skill set for ADAs, followed by interpersonal skills, work-related judgment and tactics, personal maturity, knowledge of the law and legal procedure, and presentation skills. The reason for this distribution is that the ADA may have ten cases to try in a given week, but it's possible that nine of them may "plead out" and the ADA has to try the tenth case on the first day of the week. He/she has to be prepared to try all of the cases because it is not known which ones will "plead out" and not require a trial. Thus good work habits and organization are necessary qualifications for an ADA.

Now consider the second column. Civil litigators' work-related judgment and tactics are most heavily weighted, followed by interpersonal skills, work habits and organization, personal maturity, presentation skills, and knowledge of the law and legal procedure. Civil (and other types of litigators) need to be able to think on their feet in court, to cross-examine witnesses, to change tactics on brief notice, etc. Interpersonal skills are important here because litigators shouldn't alienate court officials or jury members. Theirs is a different skill profile compared to the ADA's.

The third column shows that civil non-litigators need to have interpersonal skills, followed by work habits and organization, personal maturity, work-related judgment and tactics, presentation skills, and knowledge of the law and legal procedure. Client relations are very important with these attorneys, as are the organization of legal papers, and showing a higher level of maturity than the other two types.

The fourth column shows that paralegals must be organized, do good legal research, get along well, and have legal knowledge. They of course are trained most in office administration, records, legal research, etc., and are highly valued in law firms.

The reader may ask why knowledge of the law is not more pronounced as a job requirement. Knowledge, of course, is not a behavior although it may be inferred from a behavior. Law school is a very intense experience, and it may be that persons with high performance levels have already been exposed to the law and that their other skills are more important once they have completed law school. Sheldon Zedeck has done similar job analyses with similar results on attorneys in his studies on admission to law school (Zedeck, 2006).

Exhibit 3
Textbook or Business School Concept of Needed Key Behaviors In the Technical Manager Job

Conceptual	37%
Technical	31%
Human	32%

Exhibit 4
Performance Dimensions for Technical Managers (Weights)
(From the critical incident technique of job analysis)

Conceptual Skills and Knowledge (7.7%)
    a. Administrative decision-making and problem-solving (3.2%)
    b. Planning, organizing, controlling; anticipating problems (4.5%)
Technical Skills and Knowledge (10.8%)
    a. Technical decision-making (5.1%)
    b. Giving specific technical direction (5.7%)
Human skills and knowledge (81.5%)
    a. Emotional maturity (16.2%)
    b. Communications (15.7%)
    c. Involving employees in decision-making (11.5%)
    d. Using proper delegation (10.2%)
    f. Decision-making and judgment on personnel matters (8.3%)
    h. Giving direction (7.0%)
    i. Showing awareness of employee needs (5.8%)
    j. Coaching and correcting; development and training (4.5%)
    k. Controlling problem employees; disciplining (2.4%)

Exhibit 5
Two Plants Showing Similar Performance Dimensions for Technical Managers

Performance Dimension	Study A	Study B
Conceptual (7.7%)	7.7%	7.2%
Technical (11.1%)	10.8%	11.3%
Human (81.5%)		
a. Emotional maturity	16.2%	21.6%
b. Communications	15.7%	13.4%
c. Employment Involvement	11.5%	11.3%
d. Using proper delegation	10.2%	4.1%
e. Personnel decisions; judgment	8.3%	7.2%
f. Giving direction	7.0%	7.2%
g. Awareness of employee needs	5.8%	7.2%
h. Coaching and correcting; training	4.5%	6.2%
i. Controlling problem employees; Disciplining	2.4%	3.1%
Total	100.0%	100.0%

Exhibit 6
Broad Behavioral/Performance Dimensions for Three Types of Attorneys plus Paralegals

Dimension	ADAs	Civil Litigators	Civil Non-Litig.	Paralegals
Work Habits	35.1%	15.7%	19.9%	58.6%
Interp. Skills	28.5%	28.8%	35.5%	17.0%
Judgment/ Tactics	19.0%	34.3%	13.5%	7.0%
Pers. Maturity	9.2%	8.7%	17.3%	7.6%
Legal Knowledge	4.5%	5.7%	10.2%	9.8%
Present. Skills	3.7%	6.8%	3.6%	-
Total	100.0%	100.0%	100.0%	100.0%

SECONDARY HIGH SCHOOL TEACHERS: The last study to be presented in this chapter is that of secondary high school teachers (Exhibit 7). Senior teachers and principals were interviewed to collect critical incidents; in this study the results were compared to a breakdown of a school district's performance appraisal format. The reader will notice that the formal document used by the school system shows more planning, curricular development, learning theory, and information accuracy than does the CI study. The latter shows more classroom behavior management, student motivational strategies, "support," and parent communication. The results are not grossly different, but the CI approach reflects the "human" touch whereas the official instrument is more technical and administrative in nature. Administrative/technical performance is probably easier to measure than are "human" outcomes. Also they are not difficult to teach in a teacher's college. In today's world, classroom behavior management may be even more in demand because of high school students' increased willingness to question authority. Although delivering lesson plans is important, the management of student behavior is necessary to get students focused on subject matter. If nothing else, the CI study shows that managing student behavior may be more important than other areas on the list of teacher performances.

Exhibit 7
Comparison of Weights Given High School Teacher Behavioral Categories by Official Performance Appraisal Instrument Vs. Those Given by a CI Analysis

Major Heading	Weights Given by	
	Official Instrument	CI Analysis
1. Instructional strategies	21%	21%
2. Classroom management	21%	33%
3. Presentation of subject matter	25%	10%
4. Providing a learning environment	15%	22%
5. Professional growth and responsibilities	18%	22%
Total	100%	100%

7. ANALYSIS OF THE I/O JOB

Now that the reader has been introduced to the CI analysis of several jobs and professions, it seems appropriate to present an analysis of our own field, the Industrial/Organizational Psychologist (I/O Psychologist). The study to follow was published in the 2003 Volume of T.I.P. (*The Industrial Psychologist*). The research was conducted by board and other interested members of Texas Industrial/Organizational Psychologists (TIOP). A questionnaire and list of all I/O's residing in Texas were developed; members were assigned blocks of names randomly chosen to call via telephone to participate in the questionnaire-type survey. The same analytical method as was presented in the previous chapter was used to analyze the interviews administered over the phone with 60 psychologists. The critical incident method was used along with task analysis and key questions. As mentioned in earlier in the book, task analysis produces a different type of result than CI analysis. Task analysis leads to the discovery of key activities and time-ratable job segments whereas CI analysis tends to discover underlying skills, knowledge, and abilities required to perform those very tasks.

At the end of this chapter, a performance appraisal format will be shown followed by a detailed explanation of each key task/behavior discovered in the job analysis. The results of the study will first be presented in the following four segments: (1) common duties and tasks; (2) relating to audiences; (3) competencies; and (4) specialty areas. Data will be displayed in Exhibit 8 (A, B, C). The first one (A) will show a display of percent of subjects responding for (1) and (2) above. The second Exhibit (B) will show both percent subjects responding for (3) above plus the percent of performance dimensions obtained through use of critical incidents; Exhibit 8(C) lists the percent of participants responding to specialty areas. This is almost an exhaustive analysis of the I/O job because it shows a weighted "part of job" component, a direct questioning component, a critical incident component, and a "specialty" component.

Exhibit 8 (A)

Percent of all Subjects Responding to Questions Concerning Part of Job, Most Difficult, Most Undertrained, Most Time Consuming, and Most Critical Tasks in the I/O Job

Category	Part of Job	Most Difficult	Most Under Trained	Most Time Con- suming	Most Critical	Derived from Cis
Administr. Management	77%		7%	41%	7%	
Project Design & Mgt.	48%		2%			
Data Collection and Analysis	42%			7%		
Personnel Management	13%			3%		
Program Management	13%		7%	2%		
Making Presentations	12%		2%			
Report Writing	8%			10%		
Professional Develop.	5%					
Marketing	18%	10%	10%		7%	7%
Client Relations	20%	7%	7%		17%	23%

Exhibit 8 (B)
Percent of all Subjects Indicating CIs
in the Data Collection Process

						Derived from Cis
Marketing						7%
Client Relations						23%
Problem Solving						45%
Work Habits						37%
Integrity and Ethics						33%
I/O Knowledge						26%
Managerial Judgment						28%
Interpersonal Skills						22%
Professionalism						18%
Personal						15%
Maturity						

Exhibit 8 (C)
Percent of all Subjects Offering Responses
Derived from Specialties

Part of Job							
Teaching	37%						
Research	30%						
Individual Assessment	20%						
Coaching and Counseling	18%						
Legal Expertise	18%						
Test Development	18%						
Training	18%						
Direct Interventions	13%						

Exhibit 9
Performance Appraisal Format for I/O Psychologists
7 = well above average; 1 = well below average

Common Duties, Tasks

Administrative management (planning, organizing, administering, etc.)	
Personnel management (recruiting, selecting, training, evaluating, etc.)	
Program management (guiding and overseeing projects)	
Project design and development (developing specific programs)	
Report writing	
Data collection, analysis and diagnosis	
Personal/professional development (engaging in self-development)	
Making internal and external presentations	

Relating to Audiences

Marketing (presenting capabilities, developing proposals, etc.)	
Client relations (maintaining positive working relationships with clients)	

Competencies

Managerial judgment (leading, motivating, making key decisions, etc.)	
Interpersonal skills (facilitating, teaming, etc.)	
Professional judgment and problem-solving (analyzing, synthesizing, etc.)	
I/O Knowledge (theory, statistics, design, legal, etc.)	
Work Habits (initiative, thoroughness, preparation, documenting, etc.)	
Personal maturity (self-control, handling change and stress, etc.)	
Professionalism (addressing problems directly, taking criticism well, etc.)	
Integrity and ethics (being truthful, using proper approaches, etc.)	
Other (specify):	

Performing in Specialty Areas

Training (delivering seminars and workshops)	
Direct interventions (organizational development)	
Test development (writing items, developing tests and instruments)	
Legal Expertise (being an expert witness, researching legal questions, etc.)	
Coaching and counseling (consulting/counseling with individuals)	
Individual assessment (using tests, interviews to assess individuals)	
Teaching (teaching undergraduates/graduate students, OBM students)	
Research (conducting basic research to further development of the field	
Other (specify):	

Total

Exhibit 10
Detailed Descriptions of Performance Areas,
Behavioral Capacities of I/O Psychologists

Common Duties, Tasks

– Administrative Management: Planning, organizing, billing, collecting, filing, purchasing, documenting, "business management," communicating philosophy and guidelines, handling departmental administration, evaluating performance, representing the organization at functions, etc.

– Personnel Management: Recruiting, selecting, training one's staff, managing assigned work force, supervising and developing other psychologists, coaching and guiding staff members as they identify and address client needs.

– Program/Project Management: Guiding strategy and overseeing quality of organizational effectiveness programs, being the project manager.

– Program Design/Development: Designing and developing programs such as leadership development, succession planning, team-building, performance management, employee relations, selection systems, assessment centers, promotion systems, change management, 360 feedback, compensation systems, etc.

– Technical Report Writing: Writing clearly and effectively, using accurate and relevant information.

– Data Collecting/Analysis /Diagnosis: Designing and analyzing surveys, arranging for interviews and analyzing results, doing program evaluation, doing training needs analysis, doing organizational analysis, etc.

– Personal/Professional Development: Seeking opportunities for continuous development, asking for feedback and guidance from a mentor, attending seminars and staying current with research literature, obtaining CEU's, etc.

– Making external and internal presentations: Reporting to management, giving speeches at conferences, trade shows, conventions, and related venues, presenting information in accurate and interesting manner.

Relating to Audiences

– Marketing: Developing prospective clients, writing proposals, presenting capabilities, promoting one's organization, etc. Selling the organization and recognizing when to offer new services.

– Client Relations: Maintaining positive working relations with client organizations and personnel, maintaining communications with clients about the nature of the work and the anticipated results, delivering executive briefings in non-technical language, realizing that burying oneself in data and detail without keeping the client in the loop is inadequate consulting.

Competencies

– Managerial Judgment: Working with people, motivating staff, making personnel decisions, using appropriate leadership style to obtain quality performance from subordinates.

– Interpersonal skills: Working effectively with colleagues, integrating the ideas of others, support others in projects involving teamwork, forming working relationships, facilitating group activities, speaking comfortably with a wide variety of individuals and audiences.

– Professional judgment and problem-solving: Asking good questions, synthesizing information obtained, drawing appropriate conclusions, working effectively when there is limited budget for "collecting more information."

- Job knowledge: Showing knowledge of I/O Psychology as a discipline including methodology and legal knowledge; showing knowledge of I/O theory, practice, statistics, experimental design, data analysis, validation, and legal guidelines that affect the practice of I/O Psychology.
- Work Habits and Motivations: Showing initiative, thoroughness, preparation, self-motivation, self-starting capabilities, plus a willingness to learn. Showing conscientiousness, skill at double-checking, follow-through, avoidance of procrastination, meeting deadlines, ability to document, report editing. Being available for client support and handling "midstream" problems.
- Personal maturity: The capacity for self-control, to accept change, to operate under stress, and to avoid over-reacting to "midstream" problems.
- Professionalism: Addressing problems directly, knowing what behavior is appropriate in a professional situation and executing it, avoiding behavior that distracts the client, referring matters outside of one's capabilities, facing criticism of one's work without taking it personally.
- Integrity and ethics: Behaving in an ethical manner, representing one's products truthfully, using approaches pertinent to the requirement of the situation rather than those that might be more convenient or profitable, rejecting assignments that would compromise one's ethics, etc.

Performing in Specialty Areas
- Training: Delivering seminars and workshops, performing supervisory or management training, training on such topics as diversity, interviewing, performance management, etc.
- Direct Intervention: Performing formal interventions such as organizational development
- Test Development: Writing test items/questions, developing new instruments including selection tools and procedures, developing questions for structured interviews, developing materials and exercises for assessment centers, developing promotional exams, etc.
- Legal: Preparing expert testimony, serving as an expert witness, researching and presenting on legal questions, supporting validation systems with researched cases and the EEOC Guidelines.
- Coaching and counseling: Performing executive or management coach-

ing, counseling individual staff members or managers, helping individuals deal with personal development.

– Individual Assessment: Conducting psychological assessments of individual candidates for selection or promotion.

– Classroom Instruction: Teaching undergraduate or graduate courses.

– Research: Conducting basic research in the I/O field where the primary purpose is knowledge acquisition or theory building rather than directly satisfying client needs.

8. SELECTION

Systematic selection of employees, as is much of psychological science, is a recent development. Organizations, of course, have survived over years of human history—without systematic measurement of human traits as a hurdle for entry. The concept of "base rate" was not defined in the past. This concept, of course, relates to the percentage of persons hired from the total candidate pool without measurement of their capabilities other than informal ones. The idea of scientific psychology was to improve the performance level of persons hired so that it would be significantly greater than that obtained by the base rate alone.

The selection (or promotion) programs which the psychologist is called to create can be simple or complex, depending on the job analysis results, the nature of the problem itself, what has worked historically for the type of situation, the sample size available, the consequences of possible errors, etc. The client should be enabled to pick persons who have higher probabilities of success on some or another criterion. Examples include rated performance, training scores, actual performance (such as number of new homes sold, quality of product produced), tenure on the job, etc. Legal ramifications of the selection process are paramount, i.e., if disparate impact is possible, then some type of validity is needed on a given study. (Note: criterion, content, and construct validity are all allowed under the "Uniform Guidelines for Employment Selection Procedures," published by the EEOC, 1978.) The reader is, no doubt, aware that tests have to be justified by validity evidence if they are part of a process that shows disparate impact on minorities, females, persons of different national origins outside the U.S., persons over age 40, and persons of varying religious backgrounds and practices. Excellent discussions of employee selection techniques are to be found in Cascio (1987) and Guion (2011).

A simple selection process could be composed of a semi-structured interview plus a single cognitive test. The interview might cover teamwork, personal maturity, interpersonal skills, work approach/habits, etc. The cognitive test might be selected to predict "hard skills" such as technical learning ability, calculations skill, vocabulary, verbal reasoning, etc. Over the 70-plus years of the use of selection tests plus years of military use, more sophisticated approaches have been developed. Nowadays one can find the use of extensive job analysis done before selection techniques are chosen. Interviews are still used as measures, but they may now be structured and can be objectively scored. Paper and pencil measures are applied toward the measure of personality, work motivations, work interests, cognitive skills, and sales and supervisory knowledge. Actual behavioral exercises, group problem-solving, and situational judgment are now used to measure behavioral capacities; these are often more extensive and valid than paper and pencil exercises because they are taken "live" instead of in representational form.

This book does not cover the details of selection research or selection theory. However, it does cover case studies in which a selection or promotion exercise was designed and accomplished; it also covers results obtained from the selection (or promotion) process. Most of the research on selection has been done for Fortune 500 companies and government organizations, including the military. With very large samples, statistical significance can be reached with very low correlation coefficients between predictor and criterion. Small organizations may feel that selection research is not possible because of small sample size. Still, as the following case summary shows, small organizations can receive real benefit from small sample research, especially if follow-up studies take place.

Results from Small Sample Research

At times the selection process does not have the benefit of a large sample size, yet the need for validated instruments is there and the need for accurate selection is there. A case along these lines was presented to the author several years ago. The company was a fishing fleet in which the captain would take a crew out for several days in the hunt for a salt water fish from which fish oil and meal is derived. The boats were equipped with a tall cabin from which the captain would work. When he spots a school of fish, he instructs the crew to lower a purse-stringing net to roll off a small boat and surround the school. He gives orders as to when to make adjustments, when to begin the purse-stringing of the net, and when to lift the nets (hopefully now full) on board the main boat. There were 12 boats in the fleet, which operate off the Gulf Coast and the Atlantic seaboards. Fleet or company managers felt they could obtain better average production per boat since some of the captains obtained a fish catch that was 2-3 times that of other boats in the fleet. The boats were manned by traditional fishing village people and most had held their jobs for a decade or more, including the captains. The question became one of how does one differentiate between low and high performing skippers. The author suggested exploratory testing and began using paper and pencil tests, corre-lating them with tons of fish caught over a three-year period. None of these measures could differentiate between low and high performers and all corre-lations were non-significant. The measures included personality, work moti-vations, cognitive measures, spatial intelligence, and mechanical aptitude. There were two psychologists on the project and one finally suggested that, since the captain's job was multidimensional in terms of tasks performed (vi-sual, reasoning, operational, planning, organizing, etc.) that perhaps a multi-dimensional ability test which required manual and visual manipulation as well as math, reasoning, common sense, etc. could predict success. While the boats were in maintenance mode, the two psychologists administered the Wechsler Adult Intelligence Scale (WAIS-R) to the 12 captains. Table 5 shows a sum-mary of results obtained:

Table 5
Annual Tons of Fish Catch by WAIS General Performance Scale

N	Tons of Fish (Annual Mean over Three Yrs.)	WAIS Scores
4	4.4	112+
4	3.2	108-111
4	2.9	107 or less

The actual correlation between fish catch and WAIS score was .59, significant at p=.02. Normally one would confirm this relationship with a cross-validation sample, but the entire population of captains was included in the research and none of the workers had the tenure required by the company for an acting captain position. Thus the question for the psychologist was whether to recommend testing with the WAIS and a cut-off score of 108 or higher or whether to tell the client there was not enough data to make a recommendation. The decision was to give all facts to the client and to tell him that he would probably benefit from the test and a high cut-off score sometime in the future, when enough candidates satisfied the tenure requirement. If there was bias here, it was that the psychologists believed that the Wechsler was the right test for a multi-dimensional job from an ability point of view.

The Selection of New Home Salespersons

Another slightly larger sample was encountered in the field of new home sales. In this case, the author had been performing sales candidate assessments but with no criterion study. Finally, a criterion did become available in the form of millions of dollars of new homes sold annually. The client was a builder who was looking to increase sales of his brand within new suburban areas. He had fallen into the habit of overlooking already performed assessment results and hiring some candidates based on personal presentation, past relationship, recommendations from previous employers (some of whom were competitors), etc. To perform validation research, the author was able to obtain annual sales volume for each of 41 present salespersons. Going back to their written assessments, he rated each on the following scale without looking at criterion data:

5	Excellent chance of success
4	Above average chance of success
3	Average chance of success
2	Below average chance of success
1	Well below average chance of success.

There were probably too few subjects to do a full utility analysis here; however, the findings were statistically significant at P = .02. The client began hiring new salespersons by taking on only persons scoring 4 or 5 on the assessment results. The company was sold before a follow-up study could be conducted, but the company HR person indicated that this selection strategy seemed to be working. The new high scorers were selling in the $4-plus million category, but low scorers kept selling in the $2 million and below category.

Results from Large Sample Research

At this point, the author will offer a case study of a complex selection approach with a large sample size. In this situation, the author was asked by an operations manager and his staff if the selection process for operators could be improved. The occasion for the request was the pending installation of a modern, computerized control room at the plant. About half of the applicants, who were already field operators, would become control room operators and most of the rest would occupy the position in coming months. Given that no control jobs existed at the beginning of the project, the consultant obtained task analysis and critical incident analysis studies which had been conducted at sister plants with processes and equipment very similar to those at the target plant, which did have control room operators.

Job analyses showed performance requirements in many different categories including technical learning capacity, making economic judgments, persistence, attentiveness, follow-through, initiative, interpersonal skills, personal maturity, and being able to reason under pressured or emergency situations. The reader may be curious about the nature of some of the critical incidents. We will choose two from the category of reasoning under emergency situations. The first occurred at a large plant having a "firehouse" for pumping water to quench flames that could break out in any unit. The standard procedure during a fire was to shut down the unit and then have hoses ready in case water would be used to put out the fire (sometimes water is not indicated). In this case, the firehouse itself somehow caught on fire. Had the operator followed standard procedure, he/she would have shut down the unit before doing anything else. This, however, would have shut down the firehouse, and it would not have been able to put out its own fire. This operator was thinking (under pressure) and was able to contain the fire by *not* following standard procedure. In another case, a fire broke out at the bottom of an ethylene tower. The operator did not put it out, because if he had sprayed anticombusting material at the base of the tower the remaining burning material would have been sucked up the column, possibly causing it to explode or to shoot off like a rocket. Again, by thinking about possible outcomes during this emergency, the operator made the correct choice and simply let the fire burn at the bottom and shutting off the feedstock from the top down.

At this point, the consultant was asked by the client to research and discover the "best" selection approach for this population. It soon became clear that a work simulation measure could be constructed which would reflect the job in terms of behaviors and behavior sequences very similar to those found in the job. Examples include upstream and downstream thinking, safety awareness, tracing lines, responding to emergencies, taking initiative, etc. Since the level of experience of the candidate population would probably give some more of a head start on this test, a simulation was designed from a continuous processing plant in another industry. The final group of subtests constructed was as follows: (a) comprehension of the instructions and a factory diagram; (b) an in-basket exercise requiring the candidates to rank plant situations in terms of their importance, and (c) a trouble-shooting and problem solving exercise which requires the taking of actions necessary to keep the plant operating. This simulation was an individual exercise and did not assess the human and interpersonal skills required on the job.

A group exercise (GE) was created for the measurement of "human" skills by assessors trained in a rating process. A group of candidates would be put together to solve a problem individually and then as a group. Assessors would rate the various participants on human skills such as teamwork or two-way communications and then come to consensus on each candidate on a 7-point scale.

A third measure is a paper and pencil inventory measuring work approach, conscientiousness, and work habits. To obtain a final score, the raw scores for the manufacturing exercise, the group exercise, and the work habits test were standardized, weighted, and added together. Normally the simulation and the group exercise would each have more weight than the work habits scale. Actually this entire grouping of measures constitutes an assessment center, which is usually done on supervisory and management candidates. However, an assessment center was appropriate for these hourly candidates because of the multitude of traits and characteristics present in the job requirements. A concurrent validation was possible because performance ratings were given to the candidates after they had experienced several months on the job. Table 6 shows a distribution of final scores versus three levels of performance, "below average," "average," and "above average." The performance ratings were a synthesis of ratings made by four supervisory/staff personnel.

Table 6
Expectancy Table (Total score); N = 147
Rated Suitability to Perform the Console Job

Total Score	N	Low		Average		High	
		N	%	N	%	N	%
56.0+	37	1	2.7%	12	32.4%	24	64.9%
52.0-55.9	37	5	13.5%	11	27.9%	21	56.8%
48.2-51.9	37	7	18.9%	19	51.4%	11	29.7%
48.1-	36	20	55.5%	12	33.3%	4	11.1%
Total	147						

The reader can see that, of the 37 persons in the top score quartile, about 65% were in the high performance category and only 2.7% were in the low performance category. At the same time, of 36 persons in the bottom score quartile, only 11.1% were in the high performance category while 55.5% were in the low performance category. The multiple regression for component scores versus the criterion was about .60.

An application of this assessment center technique at another plant showed that, over a five-year period, 134 of 135 selectees passed an 8-week introductory training process. Also, of the remaining 134, 131 survived a three-year internship. One could ask "Why didn't more of them resign over the apprenticeship period?" In this particular location, plant jobs are hard to come by and there is very little voluntary turnover. Of course, not all selection programs work so well. It would seem that the more energy, research, types of testing, and breadth of job analysis one has, the better the results.

Statistical selection is a vital process for organizational performance, even when validity coefficients are a little low. Basically, none of those presented in this chapter would be considered low. Overall, there are many different types of selection processes and many different types of target audiences. As the reader will eventually discover, they are useful when used alone and also when combined with other types of organization development. A disparate impact analysis, displayed in Table 7, confirms that there were no differences between black applicants and white applicants for three plants with respect to the total scores for the assessment center.

Table 7
Disparate Impact Analysis of Three Applications
of the Assessment Center

Plant		No. Black Applicants	No. White Applicants	Mean Score, Black Applicants	Mean Score, White Applicants
A	Total Score	10	109	50.32	50.49
B	Total Score	19	252	48.78	50.19
C	Total Score	32	232	51.75	51.99

(Note: the mean scores for black/white applicants were not different with respect to statistical significance.)

EEO considerations have not been emphasized in the writing of this book. They have been considered, of course, in any selection, promotion, training, or performance appraisal project presented. It is of great importance that all validation work take disparate impact into consideration. The book could have taken the route of presenting EEO matters and cases in detail but there would be essentially no room left for the other topics such as philosophy, ethics, aesthetics, job justification, individual assessment, etc. Test statistics generated by the author have been sent to the EEOC for several clients, and there was no follow-up by the Agency. The OFCC requested all reports plus the author's testimony before a committee of local officials for a specific manufacturer and there was no follow-up by the agency.

9. EXECUTIVE/MANAGERIAL SELECTION

Probably one of the most used yet least studied type of selection is individual in nature. It is actually an older form, having been used to select salespersons more than 70 years ago. It exists in several forms, some of which are described below:

1) IN-DEPTH INTERVIEW: Here the psychologist explores the candidate's background, personal history, work history, goals, self-analysis, answers to key questions, etc. This process can take 3-4 hours and is basically an attempt to use an interview to "leave no stone unturned." If done with managerial candidates, it is accompanied with a lengthy report that concludes with a recommendation for hiring or not. If done with a present employee, it should close with ideas for development including coaching, seminars, books, tapes, plus courses on finance, human resources management, marketing, production management, project management, etc. Sometimes these assessments are used for career counseling, promotion, and placement within the organization.

2) INTERVIEW PLUS TESTS: This type of assessment relies on a shorter interview but adds such instruments as measures of work interests, personality tests, supervisory knowledge, sales comprehension, projective tests, leadership effectiveness, etc. In addition, cognitive measures are used such as critical thinking tests, vocabulary, math, numerical and symbolic reasoning tests. Such a battery can last all day but results in a very thorough analysis and also usually includes recommendations for development.

3) MANAGERIAL ASSESSMENT CENTER: This type can take up to two or three days and involve paper and pencil measures, simulations

of managerial tasks, exercises involving group problem-solving, in-basket exercises, individual interviews, etc. These are very thorough and are usually validated against multiple criteria such as job progression, goals attained, performance ratings, etc.

It turns out that managerial assessment is a key component of the I/O Psychologist's toolkit. Too often, in our society, persons not fit for leadership roles are already in them. A list of such types of persons is presented below:

1) Persons with emotional difficulties: These persons have one or another version of emotional illness or instability. This could include persons with neurotic tendencies, those with character disorders, narcissists, emotional manipulators, authoritarian personalities, co-dependent personalities, etc.

2) Persons with psychopathic or sociopathic leanings: These persons may lie about their credentials, attempt to gain credit for work not performed, construct schemes to enrich themselves at the employer's expense, choose paths that empower themselves rather than the company, etc.

3) Persons not interested: Some candidates are not really interested in managerial work but have been encouraged to "try out" for it.

4) Planners but not doers: Some can do the planning and procedural aspects of the job but are not decision-makers.

5) Lack of cognitive skills: Fairly often, candidates will appear who do not possess the intellectual ability for managerial work.

6) Theoreticians but not executors: A manager has to have the theory but also has to have his "feet on the ground." This category includes those with leadership ambitions but not much skill at execution.

When seeking good managers, it is important to avoid the selection of people whose weak points exceed their strengths. Bad management is one of the plagues of our society, and psychological assessments attempt to combat this condition. The assessments should, of course, focus on strengths as well as weak points so that high potential candidates can be identified. Chapter 6 shows the various characteristics of a full or good manager. There are various reasons why inept managers exist; a few are listed below:

1) The Peter Principal (Peter, 1969): This continues to be a useful idea; workers who have reached their level of competence sometimes are promoted to the next level, for which they have only limited capabilities.

2) Hiring the best technician or engineer: This person may or may not have supervisory or managerial capacity.

3) In some corporations, people are judged by whether they adhere to the "party line" or not. These people continue to stay in their jobs because they have conformist rather than creative personalities.

4) Promotion by tenure: In some companies, one's longevity becomes the criterion for promotion rather than potential managerial skills.

5) Family matters: Family members often receive senior positions in family-owned businesses.

Four Candidates for a Public Service Position

The next case study is about four candidates for the assistant city manager position in a city sized 350,000. The author was asked to perform executive assessments on all four during a two-day weekend. All had good references from their current manager and peer group. All were administered an extensive assessment by the author including a lengthy interview plus personality, motivational, work habits, and work interest testing. Also they were given sales and supervisory knowledge, cognitive, and critical thinking tests and asked to write a self-analysis. The city manager was the client for this assignment. He did not provide a job description or much preliminary information on the candidates. At first, the reasons for this were unknown to the author, but the city manager made clarifying statements later in the process.

It turned out that all four candidates showed typical traits and characteristics for a managerial position. None had low cognitive skills, critical thinking, or supervisory knowledge. All seemed to be personable, approachable, stable, organized, and dedicated to a career in the public service. They were all interested in leadership roles. Differences among them seemed to be in their work interests and their concept of what the job was about.

Candidate No. 1: The first candidate could do what was asked of him but in a very relational manner. He had been a city manager in a town sized 40,000 and was accustomed to treating people well, being highly sociable, and motivating people with constant encouragement and little discipline or correcting. He was very positive in outlook and had decided to enter a more rewarding career than what was offered by the smaller town.

Candidate No. 2: The second candidate was a person who probably could do the job but who would emphasize the obtaining of federal grants and the use of outside resources and consultants to contribute to city operations. He would be fair and egalitarian with personnel but not necessarily extroverted or approachable. He was currently in a federal job in Washington, D.C., and seemed interested in the city position in order to broaden his capabilities and his resume.

Candidate No. 3: The third candidate was an active city manager from a location sized 100,000 in the Midwest. In the interview, he gave examples about running departments, procuring equipment, doing performance evaluations, recruiting and hiring, etc. It became clear that this candidate was used to working with and motivating people and keeping up with daily operations. He was aware of professional responsibilities and was a member of a national city manager's association. He too was looking for a step-up careerwise and seemed to think the present city would be large enough in which he could eventually progress.

Candidate No. 4: The fourth candidate was from the West Coast and seemed to be making progress in a city about the same size as the client's city. He had served in several different departments and was used to dealing with a public union. Although he talked about his role in city operations, many of his examples were about union relationships and taking "hard" stances when necessary. He was aware that the client city was not unionized and may have wished to advance his career by having both union and non-union experience shown in his resume.

The client asked for a reporting session with the author in a couple of weeks; he wanted an outline of candidate characteristics prepared for discussion with the author. This session took about two hours to complete. The author had already guessed something about the role the new assistant city manager would have to play. Still, it seemed that the client wanted statements from the author that were not colored by the client's expectations and needs. From newspaper articles and local citizens, the author had already guessed that the atmosphere at city council was tense and that this could be a factor in the city manager's thinking.

As the meeting with the city manager progressed, it became apparent that in-fighting at city hall was very much on his mind; at this point, the assignment reached a state of clarity. The new assistant would basically be in charge while the city manager would be spending most of his time in meeting with members of city council, attempting to reduce discord, working toward goals acceptable to most members, dealing with the press, etc. The assistant had to be someone who could oversee the departments, keep people focused on their jobs, handle problems, and, in effect, operate the city on a day-to-day basis.

Once this clarity was obtained, the psychologist and the city manager (who had interviewed all of the candidates) began to close in on who would be best for the job. At first, the client reviewed candidate traits and characteristics derived from the assessments. Since all seemed to have the basic traits needed for managerial work, the matter of leadership approach was discussed. It became clear that the first candidate, who was very relational, may not have been decisive enough to operate at the larger city level. The thinking was that one can take "informal" management only so far and that the job could exceed his capacities.

The second candidate, who was very concerned about integrating federal programs into the city's projects and who was very data-driven, might tend to ignore some of the day-to-day realities of the job. To be sure, he was bright and committed, but the issue was where he would focus his effort. Also, he would probably be somewhat "distant" from the average employee.

The fourth candidate, who was skillful and approachable, was probably more concerned with career than with keeping departments afloat. Also, he seemed highly concerned with methods for dealing with unions and with winning/losing rather than basic operations and employee relations.

The third candidate, then, who showed many signs of being a good "operator," was chosen. The city manager was comfortable with an experienced manager in the job who was probably going to "get things done" while the city manager was basically absent. It helped that this candidate was currently a city manager in a fairly large town because he would have had his own city council to deal with, and would know something about what the client was going through.

Hopefully, the reader has gained something from this story. It was an intricate process for the author; what was learned was generalizable to other situations in which recruiters have produced worthy candidates who then undergo psychological assessment to deal with the fine points of the hiring process. With respect to this chapter as a whole, readers who are not trained in individual assessment should benefit from this short review of approaches and the case studies.

It is the opinion of the author that I/O psychologists who do individual assessments should have some training in clinical psychology so that they are familiar with personality factors at a "depth" level. A psychologist who is trained in employment interviewing but who is not trained in projective testing, defense mechanisms, clinical interviewing, or psychopathology may miss themes in the candidate's behavior that are worth exploring.

10. Training

Of course there is a big difference between selection and training as organizational interventions. In a training strategy, there is the hope that subjects can acquire new KSA's or attitudes; whereas, in a selection strategy, there is the hope that already existing KSA's can be discovered in applicant populations. Training requires experienced facilitators who know their field and also who know how to achieve training objectives. There are organizational problems identified as "training needs" that are not really training problems. Training may help in the sense of delivering change management skills, conflict resolution techniques, or job content skills but it does not usually address the deeper topics such as the reason for change, the source of poor attitudes, or what caused the conflict in the first place. A skilled I/O psychologist may ask for permission to perform a "root cause analysis" in order to discover underlying difficulties. In such cases, the request for training should not be taken literally if it appears that training would treat symptoms rather than causes. Sometimes the consultant can do a root cause analysis as the training process itself gets underway.

For example, the author was once involved in a team building session with operations and salespersons at a company that published magazine and newspaper advertisements. After a few sessions, the consultant asked the group to go beyond focusing on personalities and come up with other things that may be causing conflict. The group was able to construct a picture of the situation. The business was a fast growing enterprise; salespersons felt they had to grab opportunities when they came along. Sometimes they didn't produce the necessary paperwork (job tickets, etc.), which were required by operations to get a job published and sometimes they didn't ask the operations manager if there was room on the docket for "rush" orders. Operations, on the other hand, felt that they had to clear a sale before it could be put on the docket to ensure that adequate time on the presses was available. They saw the sales force as building a groundwork for commissions without much concern for the stability and ultimate profitability of the business. Salespeople saw the limits imposed by operations as not facilitating the short term growth of the business and their personal compensation. Slowly, through team-building, both groups agreed to respect the needs of the other and group sessions seemed to take on a spirit of cooperation rather than competition. In effect, then, a request for training turned into a conflict management project.

In another example, a request for "communications" training took place in a machine shop which built unique equipment and parts for a variety of industries and also government institutions. Since the parts were "one of a kind," much communication was required between shop workers, office staff, accounting, and sales. It seemed logical that "communications" training would serve this client. The consultant, however, soon realized that the owner and general manager meant to increase "listening" skills among employees so that his orders would be better understood, i.e., that downward communications would be more effectively received. The real assignment became one of continuing the meetings with employees while meeting privately with the owner on the topic of his management style and business philosophy. He was clearly a "Theory X" (MacGregor, 1960) manager who made all decisions himself. Follow-up was done periodically and eventually the owner authorized supervisory training for both his staff and himself.

If the consultant knew the owner better, he might have been able to spot the problem at the start. However, he got to know the owner during the project and the events of the project itself enabled the consultant to realize what was really happening. Ideally he would have interviewed a few employees and supervisors to get their opinions about the nature of communications at the company; however, this case seemed standard and straightforward that no preliminary work was done.

The next example is one of the legitimate uses of training as a strategy. The author was presented with the problem of lack of formal training among operators at an air separation plant. In the past, learning had taken place through unstructured OJT. Over the years, the operators seemed to have mastered the basic tasks of the job; however, there was no desire in the management group to repeat this haphazard approach. The consultant hired a technical training specialist and a task analysis was performed to arrange the job into major duty areas, many of which turned out to be equipment-specific. Modules created from training objectives written by company staff, the author, and the technical training specialist and were given titles such as "the nitrogen liquefier," the "reversing heat exchanger," or the "argon refinery." The technical training specialist and the author constructed these modules from interview notes, publications research, manufacturer's manuals, and published training manuals for the field in general. At the conclusion of the project, 20 modules had been created complete with introductory theory, the process itself, how the process was controlled, and an explanation of maintenance and troubleshooting techniques. While taking a given module, the trainee would spend shifts with a hands-on trainer who would gradually let her/him operate the equipment. Follow-up showed that the modules were being used and were achieving training objectives.

There are of course a wide number of applications of training theory and technique throughout industry. Probably one of the best practitioners was Robert Mager (1988), who urged training designers to distinguish between deficiencies in execution and deficiencies in training. If there is a deficiency in execution, then the system of rewards and punishments for reaching training objectives should be re-evaluated. If there is a deficiency in knowledge, then goal-setting should be done with specific, behaviorally stated objectives (rather than "fuzzies") and should be followed by answers to questions such as "Is practice provided?" and "Is there feedback provided"?

A professional question is whether an I/O psychologist should extend him/herself into the world of technical training. The answer is that he/she is capable of performing the necessary task analysis, have the tasks rated, and have the tasks grouped so that actual modules can be created. After that, this process requires a specialized technical trainer to write text and learning exercises. It is best for the psychologist and the training designer to work hand-in-hand throughout the project. The designer would ultimately construct the modules; together, they would construct the exams and "show me" exercises required to indicate comprehension and mastery.

Sometimes the project is very large. Years ago, the author's firm was asked to bid on a program to redesign the curriculum at the U.S. Coast Guard Academy. The firm did not obtain the project, but did receive an understanding of what was required. The Coast Guard, at this time, wanted to preserve its college majors and yet streamline some of the engineering and science topics into practical channels. Instead of teaching physics to academic majors, for example, the Academy would teach Navigation I and Navigation II. This is somewhat reminiscent of a chemical plant changing an apprentice course in chemistry to one entitled "How to Operate a Reactor." The Coast Guard project would have required psychologists, academicians, and "course" designers.

It is possible to validate training programs. In the table below, 65 of the tasks in a convenience store program were rated average or high in "importance" and average or high on "emphasis given in training."

Table 8
Rated Task Emphasis given in Training
versus Rated Importance on the Job

Task Emphasis Given	Task Importance		
	Low	Average	High
Low	10	10	5
Average	5	7	20
High	5	8	30

The Chi-square for this table was statistically significant at p = .01. Thus there is a high relationship between the task importance and the task emphasis in training ratings and one could say that the training program meets statistical requirements for validity.

Overall, training is of course a needed development strategy in organizations. It should be validated and based on actual need with adequate preliminary analysis. A request for training should be discussed and examined at the start to determine whether it is appropriate. It could be indicative of a real training need or there may be something else that is underlying the request. It is, of course, difficult to distinguish between the need for organizational change versus a request to conduct training. The consultant should listen a lot, get whatever versions he can of the organization's internal history, ask management its expectations for the best and worst possible outcomes, and contrast the differences between the technology required for training with those required for organizational change or development.

11. Unusual Assessment, Counseling and Training Situations

We are dealing with humans like ourselves in many of the interactive situations that I/O psychologists encounter. They can be refreshing for their humor, their drama, and for what they reveal about human nature. They remind us that the human spirit is alive and well and that people can reveal something of themselves as creatures rather than automatons.

First case: The author had a large, multinational client with very talented leaders in various subsidiaries. One of its companies manufactured electrical and electronic equipment and was in need of a Vice-President of Marketing. An executive search firm discovered a candidate with two previous jobs in the business; the client sent the candidate to the author for an executive evaluation. After taking tests in critical thinking, numerical reasoning, verbal comprehension, and projective tests, it became time for the candidate to undergo a lengthy interview. It turned out that the candidate had been orphaned during childhood and that he was reared by Jesuit priests in Brooklyn. Before that, he had undergone a fairly "rough" life as a homeless child in the same city. He went through elementary and high school with the Jesuits and then went to City College for a Bachelor's in Technology. Working his way through, he obtained Master of Engineering and Master of Business Administration Degrees, the latter while in the Army. He became a Ranger and was sent to Vietnam. He volunteered for a second tour as a behind-the-lines intelligence officer. He stated that, during this period, he actually grew to enjoy killing sentries, enemy intelligence people, and specific individual enemy officers targeted by his Headquarters. Upon discharge, he was treated by a psychiatrist because he had begun to feel that his life behind enemy lines was normal. He reported that a year or so of psychiatric intervention had helped him immensely in dealing with his experiences and feelings and that he was now ready to enter a normal journey in civilian life.

At somewhere near the beginning of the interview, the candidate reached down and picked up a leather "men's" purse and placed it on the table. The author ignored the purse, completed the interview, and bade goodbye to the candidate, telling him he would hear from the company in a couple of weeks. The candidate had scored extremely well on the psychometric instruments and had made the impression of a strong candidate who seemed capable of doing the job. When the author reported to the president, the latter's first question was: "What did you think of the purse?"! The author had felt perfectly happy to continue ignoring the subject because of the amount of time it would take to go into the psychodynamics; however, the client actually wanted some immersion into it because of his need to understand the behavior. The organization was a fairly conservative one, and the President sincerely felt it was inappropriate both to bring the handbag to the interview and to display it on the top of the desk. The author then proceeded with an interpretation as follows: the candidate had gone through a very tough childhood, had acquired self-confidence and a strong self-image from a disciplined Jesuit orphanage, had withstood the horrors of war "behind the lines," and had competed as a businessperson in marketing. The "purse" was most likely a symbol of independence and self-sufficiency. His message here was to make sure the client president and the psychologist understood that he was proficient in doing his job but that he was his own person who made his own decisions and who would not violate personal morals or beliefs. The conversation went on for a while, and the President seemed to understand the psychologist's interpretation. The psychologist then asked the client to double check his references and attempt to determine whether he had satisfied conservative clients in the past.

Follow up showed that the candidate from Brooklyn was not hired, and a reason was not given. One can guess that this company was not ready for such an independent person. The "finding" from the author was that this was a strong candidate who would help the company much more than hurt it over the months and years to come. If there is a lesson here, it is that the psychologist should go ahead and make his/her judgment based on standard technique and let the chips fall where they may. If the company president felt the candidate would not fit the "culture" of his organization, it was his call rather than the psychologist's.

Second Case: A semi-skilled worker was applying for a delivery job. The author and the company had developed a selection program because the job had a high responsibility level and a validity study showed that mechanical skill, intellectual ability, and a customer service orientation were required for success. As the interview drew to a close, the candidate stated that he had been shot in the back a couple of years ago but that he had recovered from the wound. The author had not asked about his physical condition at this point. The candidate went on to tell his story, i.e., that he and another person had been driving a light truck late at night and that a car drew up behind them and the people inside began shooting with automatic weapons. The candidate's companion was not hit, largely because an oversized tire was positioned between him and the shooters. The candidate, however, was hit once in the back; the gunmen left, and the candidate was taken to a nearby hospital. The question for the author was what do we make of this. In the interview the candidate had talked about being in a gang once before but those days were "gone forever." Still, it seemed possible that someone was pursuing him and attempting to assassinate him. The author decided to discuss the story with the client, whose thought was that if this person were hired, trouble could follow. He was not about to risk incidents at his business by hiring someone who may have been a gang target.

Third case: A third condition occurred during an organizational analysis of an international company. One of the key departments had been experiencing low morale, poor performance, and inadequate communication both within and also with international sites. The author interviewed all professionals in the department with the promise of giving 360 type and test feedback from executive assessments. All participants were offered information about their strengths and weak points plus ideas about workshops, tapes, and courses they could take to improve their functioning as staff members. The personal life of one of the managers had taken a turn for the worse; the person had been drinking heavily and had sour relationships with both local staff and international staff. All participants in the study received both positive and negative feedback with the idea that weaknesses could be worked on and strengths improved. The person referred to above went up the next management level to complain about the psychologist, who had treated him with the same developmental model as everyone else. The person resigned in two days.

The next step was hard to believe for the psychologist. He was called in by international management and told that it is not a custom to offer any negative feedback to employees in the company. Apparently it was held that positive training and counseling was all that was allowed in the company culture regardless of their 360 or assessment results; in fact, people were not to be reminded that weak points could be corrected. The psychologist was not used again by the company. The psychologist took issue here because a person would never know what he/she had done wrong and therefore have no basis for real correction.

Fourth case: The next situation was a learning one for the author. He was doing supervisory training with police sergeants and thought he was teaching them the skill of negative assertion, one of the skills in assertiveness training. It turned out that the sergeants knew more about negative assertion than the psychologist. It is the ability to take an insult from a protestor or marcher and to show that the policeman could handle the criticism or the insult and even ask for more, to show that they were like "water off a duck's back," i.e., that he was not being affected and that he could even handle more. This is a case in which experience is perhaps the best teacher. It fits studies of key behaviors in police work which show that cops are not reactive; instead they tend to be proactive and to handle hostility rather than return it. This "finding" is especially important today when they draw so many complaints from the general public about being aggressive or hostile. The author has been involved with two major studies of police behavior and has found that policemen normally show self-control and a strong desire to ameliorate a situation rather than make it worse.

12. PROVIDING JUSTIFICATION FOR SUPERVISORY POSITIONS

The process of justifying supervisory positions requires a fine-tuned, research approach; however, most petrochemical and other manufacturing plants rely on some type of published report which attempts to standardize worker/supervisor ratios based on surveys of multiple plants. In the petrochemical industry, the "Solomon" report (2009) serves such a purpose. A current client, however, was internally split over whether this report was actually useful and accurate. Some managers felt that the supervisors in the laboratory should be eliminated altogether and self-directed teams used instead. Others were in favor of following the suggestions of the Solomon Report, which would reduce the supervisory force by a factor of 50%. The company was interested in reducing payroll and saw this as a way to do it. A third group of managers, however, were convinced that the contribution of shift supervisors was substantial and definitely should not be eliminated and that changes in the supervisory work force would only increase costs rather than reduce them.

The consultant was asked to investigate the situation and come up with his own recommendation as to how the company should proceed. There were seventeen "analysts" or entry level technicians in the laboratory, which provided the plant with the chemical testing of a variety of intermediate and final products. The main tests had to do with whether various hydrocarbons and associated chemicals met specifications.

Project Design

It was clear that data collected on this supervisor issue should provide a strong argument one way or another. Current economic conditions in the industry were not good, and a conclusion to keep the supervisors would have to be pretty much beyond dispute. The author decided that multiple approaches would shed more light on the problem; if these were convergent, the result would be a stronger back-up for whatever conclusions were drawn. The studies/approaches used are listed below:

(1) Interviews with plant managers, laboratory managers, shift foremen, laboratory analysts, laboratory technicians, blenders and product inspectors: These interviews focused on the functions served by the foremen, the reasons for these functions, types of utilization of the foremen, the interaction of the foremen with the laboratory management information system, critical incidents among the foremen population, the possibilities of job redesign, and related topics.

(2) Continuous work sampling: The consultant visited the foremen at randomly selected times (including night hours); some questioning took place, i.e., "What are you doing now?"; "Why are you doing this?" Each of these visits was for two hours and the consultant took continuous notes of the foreman's activity during each sampling period.

(3) Work Diaries: Each foreman kept a work diary for a period of five days, listing tasks and subtasks performed along with the approximate percent of daily time spent on major task groupings.

(4) Task Analysis: Each task uncovered by the job analysis so far was listed by major duty category; incumbents and managers were asked to rate the tasks on a seven-point scale indicating "time spent."

(5) Opinions from unit leaders whose functions were served by the laboratory: These individuals had the perspective of how the laboratory participated in problem-solving in the units, shedding light on differences between unit readings and laboratory readings, the possibility that the samples sent to the lab were faulty, what might be the cause of an off-spec reading, etc.

(6) Benchmarking: Given that the Solomon Report authors did benchmarking at other companies, an attempt to produce a more in-depth look at other companies was accomplished. Ten similar plants were contacted and asked to participate in a benchmarking study in return for a copy of the study results. Ten local laboratory managers were asked to discuss their approach to laboratory supervision plus other characteristics of their laboratory which could influence supervisory workload.

Results from the various studies listed above were extensive and will be summarized below.

Interviews and Task Analysis: These are the general duties performed, with approximate time spent percentages in parentheses.

(1) Directing and Operating the Laboratory (22%)
(2) Managing laboratory personnel and maintaining safety (19%)
(3) Maintaining plant and external communications (18%)
(4) Monitoring equipment and building maintenance; misc. functions (15%)
(5) Monitoring product movement and shipping (14%)
(6) Performing quality control functions (12%)

Continuous Work Sampling: Of ten hours sampled, results showed activity in all areas uncovered by the task analysis; of most importance, there was virtually no "idle" time spent. The supervisors did not seem to be increasing their activity levels because of being observed because most of the stimuli for task initiation came from the outside, the telephone, other people in the lab, etc. The supervisors had time for computer and records work only when not being called to do something else.

Work Diaries: The supervisors tended to clump work into categories when they completed their diary pages at the end of the day. These results enabled the researcher to estimate approximately the amount of time given to each category. This was compared to the "time spent" ratings given to tasks in the task rating study.

Opinions from Unit Leaders: These leaders discussed the role of the supervisor in problem solving at the unit level (as discussed above); they also listed what seemed to be the pressures on the job, given that they were in daily contact with the supervisors. These pressures are listed below:

1. The current overload
2. The current need for more samples, testing, and people

3. The dangers of backlogs
4. Work requested by other plants
5. Constant upgrades on the laboratory management information system
6. The fact that that the laboratory is running thousands of tests and that one bad result could be critical
7. Current tank storage is inadequate
8. Some equipment is antiquated
9. Product changes occur at least twice in a 12-hour period
10. Attempts to cut sample load are not realistic
11. There is no time for repetitive testing
12. The unit engineers are always changing test orders
13. Current lab techs and analysis are stretched out on overtime
14. New storage units are going to require increases in raw material and unit testing
15. There are new agencies to report to
16. If the lab gets saturated with orders, it will have to turn down work
17. Someone has to stay "on top" of the whole sampling and testing situation
18. There is a need for a mediator among laboratory customers to determine who has priority
19. There is a need for someone to monitor speed of sample processing and to do monitoring of process streams
20. There is a need for advanced interpersonal skills in the supervisor as he/she deals with a myriad of customers, operations people, regulators, product inspectors, etc.
21. There is a need for someone who can make decisions, live with the results, who can influence key people without confrontation, who can discipline when necessary, who can call people out on overtime even though it is an inconvenience, and who can take the initiative to investigate a profile of test results that does not "look" right.
22. There is a need for someone who can make judgments on the quality of data obtained, who can recommend re-sampling when necessary, and who can communicate the accuracy of a test to a unit.
23. There is a need for someone to take on the legal responsibility for signing key documents, especially those authorizing a load for shipment.

The Benchmarking Research: Ten other plants (including competitors) were surveyed with respect to their lab supervisor situations. The median number of product barrels/day was 260,000; the median number of hourly employees working in the lab was 24 (note: the client had more barrels/day and fewer hourly employees). The median number of tests run per day was 1200, whereas the client ran 1700. The number of plants with a shift foreman set-up was 4 of the 10. They were happy with their situations. Five of the plants did not have shift supervisors; none of their lab managers, however, were satisfied with their situations. Only one of the ten had a non-supervisor set-up and was happy with it. Results from the benchmarking research, then showed that a supervisor situation was more preferable than a non-supervisor one.

The point made by the investigation as a whole, then, offered the conclusion that, had the Solomon statistical report been followed, the basic nature and value of the supervisory job would have been overlooked. Based on what incumbents do and the problems they handle, it is not realistic to ask them to walk away and leave what would be pieces of the job in the hands of technicians or self-directed teams. These would still be responsible for running tests plus operating the laboratory as a whole. All data and interview research were convergent on the point that the supervisory job was essential to the plant operation.

13. Supervisory Promotion

One of the most practical areas of concern in industry is supervisory selection or promotion. Unfortunately, it is still the case that the "best worker" is promoted with no real systematic effort made to choose someone with actual supervisory skills. Another variant of "traditional promotion" is for the most liked person to get the job (rather than the most competent).

The Good Ol' Boy Approach

In a specific case known to the author, a light manufacturing client had ten plants operating in separate geographical areas. The author was asked to assess possible replacements for the plant manager position at each place, given that the plants were declining in production and that some of these potential candidates might actually replace managers who had been on board but whose production was in decline despite there being no changes in the market. The potential replacements, one from each plant, were assessed by measurement of critical thinking, cognitive ability, interests, work habits, personality, and supervisory knowledge. Results showed that only one of these candidates showed competitive critical thinking and cognitive scores. All, however, scored well on interpersonal skills, personality variables, verbal fluency, and supervisory knowledge. The inference was made by the client and the consultant that the possible replacements (including Assistant Plant Managers, Superintendents, and Supervisors) were not delivering in areas requiring conceptual, analytical, and cognitive areas skills but were probably doing well in maintaining a friendly and supportive atmosphere. To use the vernacular, they were "good ol' boys" who got along with everyone but who might not deal effectively with the tough operations, maintenance, and accounting problems faced by the plants. The result of the testing led to a "hold" on promotions; meanwhile another approach to supervisory selection was being developed and will be presented in the next case study.

A Systematic Approach to Supervisory Selection

First, it is instructive to review various types of supervisory selection as follows:

(1) Best worker or "gets along with everybody" approach
(2) Interview only (sometimes completely informal)
(3) Best regulatory record (lack of absenteeism, safety record, disciplinary record, etc.)
(4) Relevant College semesters completed
(5) Results of cognitive testing; critical thinking
(6) Combination of biodata, personality, work habits, and judgment
(7) Assessment center
(8) Performance as temporary supervisor
(9) Combinations of the above

The list above is not universal; it is presented to show various formulations that a program could take. Included above are the "best worker" approach and the "gets along with everybody" approach. Now, after years of experimentation, the author is ready to recommend an approach that has unique characteristics because of a combination of three factors. It is presented in the case below.

The case involved a petrochemical plant with a stated need to objectify maintenance and operations supervisor promotion processes. The author has developed a preference for measuring background, personality traits, and personnel judgment in a single predictor, the Supervisory Profile Index (SPI, ePredix, 2004). Each of the 180 items in the SPI was validated separately; this item specific approach to validation was performed by the Index's original author, RBH, Inc. Also the test had been validated as a complete entity against ratings and promotional criteria. The SPI is a paper-and-pencil approach which is more than adequate; additions to it, however, have the potential to increase predictive power.

The next step was to borrow a segment from assessment centers, namely the Group Exercise, which was presented in Chapter 8. In a couple of group activities with defined tasks, one can assemble about six candidates at a time and three trained assessors can rate individual behaviors in such categories as communication, group problem-solving, and teamwork. After these ratings were done, then the assessors went through a consensus process and each candidate was scored on an overall 7-point scale.

The third component of the process was a performance appraisal on each candidate done by multiple judges. The performance instrument covered four behavioral dimensions known to be required in both the hourly job and the supervisory job, and can be listed as follows:

(1) Demonstration of technical knowledge
(2) Work habits and motivations
(3) Interpersonal skills
(4) Personal maturity

Rating dimensions used to assess the four behavioral/knowledge dimensions above were constructed and given to two present supervisors who knew the performance of the candidate. They made copies of their questionnaires and passed them to each other and to two higher-level (managerial) personnel who were generally familiar with the candidates' performance. After each had read the others' performance notes and ratings, they engaged in a group discussion with a psychologist present to facilitate objectivity.

At this point, raw scores for all measures were converted to T scores and added together for an overall score with each measure equated to 1/3 of the total. Table 9 shows a distribution of the T score combinations for a group of candidates. Validities of the exercise and SPI measure are shown in Table 10. Persons scoring above the "break" in the distribution in Table 9 were promoted. A three-year follow-up showed that each person in the promoted group was still with the company and had received a "meets minimum standards" requirements designation and most were high average or above. All three of the measures met the EEOC requirement for "searching for alternative measures" (they were not cognitive measures).

Table 9
Distribution of Combined Scores
for the Supervisory Selection Process

Standard Score	f
57-58	1
55-56	2
53-54	4
51-52	4
49-50	-
47-48	4
45-46	2
43-44	2
Less than 43	3

Table 10
Correlations of the G.E. and the SPI with Ratings
Of Supervisory Personnel

Measure	Ns	First Usage	Second Usage	Third Usage
Group Ex.	22/41/60	.44**	.43**	.29**
SPI	22/41/60	.36*	.39*	.29**

**p=.01; *p=.05

14. CONSUMER RESEARCH

From time to time, practitioners are asked to perform projects in which consumer opinions are measured and used as a guide for decision-making. This is a subset within the province of the I/O field because it is taught in graduate school, it involves data collection from people, attitude measurement is used, interpretation of results can be complex, and it can involve "image" research. We have already covered one example of "touching base" with the external environment in the benchmarking study mentioned earlier in the book. Now we will cover several examples of this type of research to offer to the reader a "flavor" of what can go on in this world of consumer psychology. We will briefly describe cases involving mystery shopper research, the use of advertising, focus groups centered on products, views of professional services by those who would be procuring the services, and questionnaire research on large items as viewed by consumers. The author has also participated in city planning studies and research in association with professional city planners.

Mystery Shopper Study

The president of a local savings and loan association came to the author for thoughts about the condition of his S & L. Measurement of the effects of local advertising had shown that the S & L was number two (#2) in the city in terms of name recognition and yet was number seven (#7) in terms of "repeat business." There were at least fifteen S & L companies in the city at this time. Interpretation of these findings could mean that customers were aware of the institution and were perhaps trying it out yet were not coming back for more of the services offered. The president needed to know why people were tending to not come back after an initial experience with branches in the chain.

After a good deal of conversation, the president and consultant agreed on the need for more data to hopefully explain the discrepancy between name recognition and repeat business. They designed a "mystery shopper" study in which six people would visit 10 S & L branches plus as many branches in two separate competing S & L's. Six shoppers would, then, visit a total of 30 branches. The task of each mystery shopper was to purchase a single $100 savings certificate at each site visited. Each shopper visited all three institutions at several branches; none were told the identity of the client. Each shopper was given a questionnaire to complete immediately after each visit. It contained the following types of items:

1. Time in minutes and seconds from the moment of entering the branch until the moment at which they were spoken to by a teller.
2. A rating of the extent to which they were shown or told relevant details about the institution and the product.
3. A rating of the extent to which the branch's representative was thorough in answering questions of any type about the S & L and its services.
4. A rating of the friendliness and approachability of the teller serving them.
5. A rating of overall satisfaction with their experience at the branch.

The shoppers, of course, were reimbursed for the certificates purchased and were paid an hourly wage for their time spent on the project. Results showed that the client's branches (as a group) were significantly higher than the competition on "Time it took to be served" and were significantly lower on the various ratings on the adequacy of the tellers' service behaviors.

This leadership council, if you will, next agreed to offer specific customer relations training to employees and began to communicate that the service aspects of the institution were as important as were the technical factors involved in running a branch. After two years had passed, the repeat business (in terms of number of transactions) went up.

Choosing between Two Ads for the Same Service

A geological and geophysical services company was interested in getting more awareness of its name in scientific journals read by geologists. They had commissioned an advertising and graphic arts firm to develop approaches; this firm settled on two presentations as follows: (1) a cartoon-like ad which showed professionals having a good time at their work and (2) a pleasant country scene showing geologists at work in the foreground. The company was having difficulty choosing between the two approaches and came to the author for an attempt at resolution. A proposal was developed whereby both ads would be shown to a population of geologists/geophysicists and rated on various dimensions including overall attractiveness (overall positive/negative "feeling") towards both ads. An ABBA presentation was done by assistants hired to perform the task of showing the ads to 60 subjects drawn from lists in the possession of the client (the services company). Results showed that the two approaches were in a "dead heat" as to overall attraction. The subjects were able to discuss the ads and talked about the "modern" nature of the cartoon ad and the "conventional" nature of the country scene. However, their aesthetic perception of the ads didn't seem to influence their actual final ratings. The client was told that the ads were equally likely to draw readers. At this point the client decided to use both ads on a random basis in several technical journals. Hopefully the client was satisfied that the ads it had commissioned would be two "best attempts" to engage the market.

Market Research for a Shopping Center

The author and members of his firm were approached by a minority entrepreneur who had conceived a plan to create a neighborhood shopping center in one of the Mexican-American "barrios" (neighborhoods) in a large city. The main question for the entrepreneur was whether there was an actual market for such a center at a specific location. A project was commissioned, and the author, an economist, and several interviewers were proposed to work on the project. After several preliminary interviews were accomplished, including a lengthy encounter with the entrepreneur, a questionnaire was developed to assess present buying patterns, daily shopping habits, means of transportation available, product preferences, and what kinds of outlets and locations would be convenient for the inhabitants. One hundred interviews were conducted in the estimated market area of the property being considered.

The researchers obtained sales/square foot averages for varieties of communities from the publications of the Urban Institute. They also physically measured square footage of pre-existing stores in the area. They determined typical market sizes by visiting current centers in various parts of town.

Results showed that the targeted area was underserved by current scattered stores. Area residents were accustomed to walking to purchase consumer goods and services. They preferred a shopping area where options were close to one another (i.e., grocery store, drug store, clothing outlets, barber shop, etc.). Using all resources possible, the center was able to secure some "anchor" tenants, to obtain extra financing (partially from neighborhood renewal organizations), and to construct the shopping center as the bottom floor in a fairly new multi-purpose building in the area. There was no formal "follow-through" except that the members of the author's firm, for the next few years, would visit the center and see that "anchor" stores were still there and that tenant turnover was minimal.

Market for Architectural Services

At one point in the development of concepts for structuring architectural services a design/build (also called a construction management) model was "invented" and used by several large firms. The idea was that architects would supervise designers, architectural draftspersons, construction managers, and marketing personnel all within the same firm. Under this model, architects would become managers rather than designers, draftsmen, or craftsmen. One firm in particular which designed schools, large buildings, hospitals, and shopping centers was seriously concerned about whether the new model was right for their clients or not. The firm commissioned the author and two colleagues to help them answer the question.

After a lengthy discussion with the client, a customer interview was designed to obtain opinions from top managers in 100 different organizations who had purchased the services of architects in the past. The market was segmented into types of building systems served (i.e., commercial, public schools, hospitals, etc.) and appointments for interviews were made by telephone to cover a 5-week time span for the research.

Most of the questions related to the major topic of "What they wanted from architectural firms" plus what they had been satisfied or dissatisfied with in the past. The executives were also asked to rate the ten largest architectural firms in town. The client was placed among the ten but it was not made known to the interviewees in terms of actual identity. They were told that their ratings and answers to questions would be kept confidential, even from the client, who would be informed by receiving aggregated results put together by the consultant.

It turned out that the survey results were of great value to the client. They showed that the market for services was very unfavorable to the construction management or the design/build model. The persons interviewed wanted architects to continue in the roles of design, maker of production drawings, and construction inspection. Their comments indicated the architect should be a designer and construction superintendent type of professional rather than a manager of various services. These consumers indicated a high degree of dissatisfaction with the modern concepts because they did not believe the architect was really competent as a design/build or a finance or marketing expert. They also rejected the idea of assembling architects who would strive to win design competitions.

For the most part, the market wanted architects to return to classical roles and focus on their technology rather than general business offerings. Follow-up was performed with this client after four years had passed. The firm had retained the classical model and was very successful with it. Sales had quadrupled over this period and the firm was highly satisfied with the choice it had made.

The Market for Middle-Class Housing

Another market survey was of the potential customers for middle-class housing. The research problem was to determine whether so-called California-style housing would be accepted in the market of another state. Focus groups were used to determine the dimensions whereby the interior and exterior of both California and traditional were being evaluated by the market. A questionnaire was constructed for persons in the market for a new home, as determined by the auto license plates of automobiles parked in front of model homes. This process identified 75 people so qualified; they were called for oral administration of the questionnaire after stating they were actually in the market. They were promised individual autonomy and told that their answers would be grouped together with those of other participants. A summary of results showed that two of the California-style models were accepted. These had a cathedral ceiling, a step-down living area, a combined living room/kitchen, and extensive use of glass walls. The builder went ahead and put the acceptable two models in new subdivisions in two cities. Follow-up indicated that the builder was satisfied with the sales results.

Consumer and survey research is well within the professional model of the general practitioner. Often the client wants to know about his image, market potential, or the possible impact of a new science or product. Opinion polling is also well within this category of professional activity.

15. VOCATIONAL COUNSELING
AND CAREER DEVELOPMENT

Typically, colleges and a few high schools attempt to counsel students with respect to choice of colleges, major, and career direction. Harrington & Hall (2007) are applied psychologists who address vocational topics and Richard Bolles (2014) was a practical adviser who addresses career choice and change. Bolles is the author of the *What Color is Your Parachute* series; he continued to revise his book annually for many years. It is the major source of self-knowledge exercises, career information, and techniques for exploration in the field we would call "vocational or career development." Below are listed various approaches to career development and something about each.

College counselors, of course, have the formal responsibility to assist students by giving them knowledge of their vocational potential. They suffer from the lack of exposure to the world of work since most have been continuously employed in a college or university staff position. Bolles (mentioned above) offers excellent self-appraisal techniques and world-of-work knowledge, but his process suffers from a lack of standardized instruments. Another approach to career development is entitled the Johnson-O'Connor Technique. It has satisfied clients; it differs in that it incorporates private tests and instruments that are not open to review to persons in the field. The approach offered by the present writer would be called "Vocational Assessment" and is composed of the following elements:

1. A life diary written by the counselee.
2. A lengthy interview performed by a psychologist with consulting experience in several industries.
3. Standardized testing of the person's personal traits including work interests, work motivations, personality dimensions, general values,

leadership style, general abilities, and supervisory and sales comprehension.

4. Standardized cognitive tests including logic, math, verbal reasoning, fluency, general aptitude, visual skills, etc.

5. Projective tests such as the TAT or sentence completion tests as appropriate.

There are several advantages to standardized testing. One is that the test-taker's profile can be compared to those of a large number of persons in a multitude of jobs. If the test-taker seems to have managerial or professional ambitions, it can be determined whether she or he is intellectually competitive with those higher level jobs. Results provide frames of references and serve to guide the process rather than reach absolute definitions of career paths. The most specific determinations can be made on those work interest scales validated on individual jobs (such as mechanic, buyer, administrative assistant, physician, financial manager, etc.). When all qualitative and quantitative data are collected, the psychologist can "pull" it together into factors (groups of scores and judgments) that define characteristics of persons being assessed.

The First Case

Our first example is that of a bank employee who was a bank operations supervisor but was considering changing to a lending job in another department. After testing and evaluation, the psychologist developed a set of "factors" that could be determiners of career satisfaction and scored his present job versus the new one under consideration on the set of factors below. The scores are the degree of "fit" between the factor and the job. A "-" is equal to minus one point, a "√" is equal to zero points, a "+" equals one point and a "++" equals two points. The factors are strengths as determined by the assessment and the psychologist. The scores are the degree of "fit" between the factor and the job. For example, the candidate shows high enjoyment of order and organization. The psychologist made the judgment that this trait would be more important in the Supervisor job than in the Lending job.

Factor	Bank Supervisor	Lending Job
Supervisory knowledge (high)	++	√
Basic work habits (good)	++	+
Interpersonal skills (high)	+	++
Raw intellectual power (High)	√	+
Visual orientation	+	√
Financial work interests (high)	++	√
Sales comprehension (high)	√	+
Enjoyment of order, organization (good)	+	√
Personal history	+	√
Total	10	5

In this case, the bank employee's boss gave him the choice of progressing either up the marketing/lending or the bank operations ladders. At first, the person was "taken back" by the multiple opportunities. Next, however, he decided he was committed to the bank and would seek out sources to help him make the choice. The psychologist recommended the bank operations path, and the person did in fact take that choice. Follow-up in six months showed he was happy with the choice and was looking forward to a career in which he would "run" a branch bank or have a HQ job in bank operations.

The Second Case
The author was coaching a second-year MBA student with experience in the petrochemical industry. He was an accountant by education and now was in the financial management group of his employer. It was suggested he take a career or vocational assessment and he seemed eager to comply. He wanted to enter the CEO ladder but agreed to have his factors scored as a potential CFO as well. His "matches" on the pertinent factors are displayed below:

Factor	CEO	CFO
Energy level (low)	—	√
Assertiveness (low)	—	√
Work interests	√	++
Work habits (good)	√	+
Supervisory knowledge (Avg.)	√	√

Interpersonal skills (Avg.)	-	√
Cognitive abilities (Avg.)	√	√
Detail orientation (High)	√	+
Personal History	-	+
Total	-3	5

In this case, negative numbers were used because some factor scores went below average. As is shown, the CEO path may not fit because of the subject's lower energy level, assertiveness, interpersonal skills, and basic cognitive skills. Also his personal and job background seemed more compatible with the CFO than with the CEO choice. The CFO path may be preferred because of his good work habits, matching work interests, personal history, and detail-orientation. On the weighting system above, the CFO is 8 points higher than the CEO factor scores.

The conclusion was difficult for the student to accept because he "looked up" to company presidents and felt the CFO job was somehow of less desirability. However, by the third counseling session, the student was asking questions about the CFO role and seemed to have "warmed up" to the idea. Follow-up was not possible in this case, but a good guess is that he focused on the financial ladder rather than the presidential ladder.

Basically, then, vocational assessment is well within the province of I/O psychologists. It may be done for placement purposes (as in the cases above), for outplacement, for internal career development in a company that wants to match the employee's perspective with that of the company, and as a service for the general public.

16. A Long-Term Client Relationship

There are clients with whom the consultant forms a long-term relationship after performing an initial assignment. The scope of work simply grows with client need as the consultant grows in understanding of client dynamics. Such was the case when the author encountered a cement manufacturer with more than 10 plants; the first encounter by the consultant was to travel to each plant, interview all supervisory and management personnel, and to come up with thoughts and ideas about improving union relations. The initial assignment was to include in the interviews the topics of the work environment, organizational climate, morale, "people" problems along with the state of labor relations. This initial project took about 3 months, including travel by the consultant.

Although top management was accustomed to mid-western culture and values, it had to visualize how different regional cultures within the company were affecting daily work life, communications, interpretation of policy, organizational norms, etc. At the California plant, for example, people tended to feel that their "rights" were very important; many had come to California because of the state's image of having an employee-oriented climate. The plant manager felt that the company had to live up to this image of "rights" being perhaps more important than any other benefit.

At the Midwestern plants, there was a tense relationship between company and union. Some workers "acted out" their hostility. At one plant, for example, bullet holes were found in the front bumper of the plant manager's car. At another, an ax blade had been jammed into a very long conveyer belt and had split the belt for about a mile of operation. At a third plant, a sack of cement had "fallen" off the top of a silo, missing the plant manager by about 10 feet.

One of the frustrations of the union members was new (forecasted) pay cuts as would be provided for in a new contract. Management responded by publishing the fact that South Korea could deliver cement on a U.S. dock cheaper than the company cement plant located at the same destination could put it there. The union, however, was not moved by this assertion.

A visit to a particular plant in the Southwest showed that there was a serious conflict between the operations and the maintenance department there. The maintenance workers would, on a daily basis, remove piles of cement dust and repair the pumps. Operations, the next day, would run the pumps beyond their capacity and build mounds of cement dust for maintenance to clean up and fix the pumps again. The consultant saw the need for a "root cause analysis" and quickly discovered that the plant was up for sale and was being "run into the ground" in order to fill quotas which were basically unattainable. Clearly, production needed to cut back so that repairs could keep up. Also, new equipment was needed to keep the plant running, but management refused to make such expenditures, hoping instead to "sell" the plant "as is."

When the consultant reported to the VP of Manufacturing on this particular plant, he seemed to take a defensive posture; he apparently was caught between the company's decision to not repair the plant and the low morale of the local workers. Rather than solve the problem, the plant was sold in a year or so, as had probably been intended by the company's long term planners.

Over the Long Haul

The consultant worked for the company over a fifteen-year period as a general psychologist who would be given various problems to work on by the Manufacturing Function and the Human Resources Department. For example, changes in the kiln fuel were made as a substitute for coal. Waste Fuel, such as used motor or transmission oil, would be sprayed into the kiln to ignite and raise the temperature so as to be able to melt limestone and various additives into a compound called "clinker." Changes required were chemically monitored, and this required the hiring of more cement chemists. Waste fuel would have better effects on the environment than would coal.

In a particular year, the change to waste fuel took place in a plant that was facing a market downturn for its cement. There were signs that the plant manager was facing a personal "burnout" situation. A visit with the plant manager confirmed that he was under stress and also revealed another source of stress. A few years ago, his spouse had been murdered by an intruder in the couple's home. A month later, in the present, the consultant was called back to visit the manager at a psychiatric hospital to which he had committed himself. The visit was at the request of the VP of Manufacturing, who was concerned about his manager in general and also concerned about whether he could function at the same level once he completed psychiatric treatment. The psychiatrist in charge felt he could re-enter the company work force but not at a level which would overload him with managerial responsibilities. Follow-up in a few months showed that the company had offered him a job as a project engineer in its technical division. An engineer by education, he had accepted and was performing well in the new role.

The consultant coached other plant managers, some because they were struggling and others who seemed to need a "sounding board" for their ideas. At one plant in particular, new ideas for employee selection were developed, validated, and carried out. The plant manager here was aggressive in the arena of labor relations. He was quick to discipline individual violations of the labor contract. At the same time, under encouragement from the consultant, he sought to establish communication with the labor leaders and he was asked to speak at the union hall, which was a "first" for this plant. The chief topic was wages, with the company saying it could no longer afford biannual increases. At other plants the union was threatening a lockout if its demands were not met. The company was preparing a back-up workforce. It turned out, however, that the union did not strike and came back to work without "walking out." Quickly, work progressed under "implemented terms and conditions," a legal procedure written by the Department of Labor which governed the relationship between the company and the union in the absence of a contract. This type of relationship existed for a couple of years until the two parties eventually came back together.

Within the company, the consultant worked on problems as they arose. For example, employees at the rock quarry at one of the plants were becoming less cooperative, more demanding, and less communicative. These problems seemed to be independent of union difficulties that might still be lingering. The quarry at a cement plant is an area in which limestone is mined. Very large equipment is used to dig and transport this raw material to a rock crusher which reduces large pieces to more manageable ones. The smaller pieces are moved by lengthy conveyor belts to the plant proper, which mixes other materials with the limestone so that it can be entered into the red-hot rotating kiln and transformed into "clinker," as referred to earlier in the chapter, which is ground into cement.

From a worker point of view, it is fairly routine for individuals in the quarry to become isolated. Each has a heavy duty machine to operate, including front-end loaders, crushers, belts, etc., and the consequences of an accident could be fatal. In the particular quarry (plant) referred to here, job attitudes had slipped to a very low point, and the company felt it was doing all it could to make the work tolerable, but couldn't change the basic tasks, equipment, or worker responsibilities.

After consulting with the plant manager and the VP of Human Resources, the author prepared a team building seminar which would address communications, skills, job attitudes, and verbalization of complaints so that real issues could be discovered rather than those which simply "blamed the company for everything."

After six 3-hour sessions were held with 11 quarry employees, the most vocal (three people) had not toned down their rhetoric. The remaining eight, however, seemed to be serious participants. The consultant came to believe that a few chronic complainers were the cause of communication and collaboration difficulties between the quarry and the plant administration. After the consultant gave a report, local management decided to wait and see whether the influence of the three complainers was diminished. It turned out that no other interventions were necessary. A six-month check revealed that quarry operations were proceeding normally and that poor attitudes seem to have been mitigated or at least lost their impact.

Over the 15-year time period of this long term assignment, psychological assessments were performed on candidates for management and high level staff positions. Follow-up ratings on those hired showed a picture of statistically significant relationships between assessment "grades" and overall performance ratings done by top level manufacturing executives.

The events of the consultant interventions over the 15-year period are offered as a model in a geographically distinct, multi-plant setting. In annual visits to the plants, the consultant was able, by interviewing plant managerial and supervisory staff, to keep up with such issues as labor relations, plant morale, the effects of equipment and process changes, and the progress of individuals. As stated above, other types of intervention were undertaken including hourly selection, team building, executive coaching, etc. The VP of Manufacturing commissioned and oversaw this process. He and the consultant were on similar learning curves as he asked the consultant to perform various tasks/projects, to receive relevant information from them, to recommend changes, and then to assign the consultant to the next logical project.

The consultant was not asked to be an in-house "spy." He was introduced at each plant, and all persons contacted were informed that they could choose not to participate with no consequences. They were also told that any information they chose to pass on during the interviews would be in the province of the VP and the consultant alone. The position taken by the VP was that the company was relatively "flat" in structure with no managerial levels between HQ and the plants. Therefore, he needed to have a way to work with the plants, to become more aware of their difficulties, and to install new HR ideas once trust was established between the plants and the consultant.

In this case, some of the advantages to the company of having a single, long-term consultant were as follows:

1. The consultant grew in his knowledge of the company and the business and was eventually able to converse with local personnel in their own "language."

2. As each year passed, trust of the consultant increased to the point that real issues could be highlighted without fear of retaliation.

3. The projects were less costly than would have been the case of using a large consulting firm with sizable corporate overheads built into their billing structures.

4. In the case of a large consulting firm, there is generally no guarantee that the same individual or individuals would be used from year to year. This is so because large firms move people around and the same individuals may not be available from year to year.

5. The client company executive does not have to become adjusted to the style and professional beliefs of the consultant on a frequent basis, as he would with ever-changing large firm consultant personnel.

6. Having the consultant do personal, frequent visits of the plants enables him/her to take "status readings" (through interviews) of constructs such as "morale," "communications," "functionality," etc.

17. GUIDANCE FROM LITERATURE, FILMS, AND AESTHETICS

You have heard it said that "Everyone is a psychologist." This can mean that everyone has common sense at their disposal, that a person with limited training in psychology has an understanding that some persons have more job performance skills than others (employee selection), that one can be trained on the "human" aspects of a job, or that people can be taught how to get along with each other, etc. It is also true that many artists including dramatists and filmmakers have a lot of insight into human motivation, why communication fails, how mentors help others, how politics works, etc.

The overlap between aesthetics and psychology can be seen in drama, films, TV series, portraits, novels, etc. Films and dramatic productions come to mind such as *The Office, Death of a Salesman, Rollerball,* and *Platoon.* Novels include *The Good Earth* and *Giants in the Earth.*

The *Office* (2005-2013) shows how the organizational dynamics of a modern, autocratic climate can be described as a comedy about one of today's dysfunctional business organizations. *Death of a Salesman* (1985, both a film and a play) is about the negative self-concept developed by a salesman whose life is based on a marketing orientation. Unfortunately, the main character (the salesman) has given up his personhood, if you will, to the idea of being successful but is not able to market his product/services. In the play, a tragedy, the main character (Willie Loman) commits suicide because he has no basis for his identity other than the sales dream. It is reminiscent of persons in organizational life who base their identity solely on their job or their ability to persuade, not including their family, religion, community, or recreational activities.

In the first edition of the futuristic film, *Rollerball* (1975), corporations have merged to the point of having single entities with titles such as "Energy," "Food," "Power," "Transportation," "Communications," etc. They have discovered that society can be ruled with universal positive reinforcement of most human needs. To use an extreme example, a high status person can ask for a new spouse if he/she is dissatisfied with the old one. One additional requirement, however, is that members of the society can be kept at peace by attending violent sports games, perhaps like today's hockey or football. The corporation invents a game called "Rollerball," somewhat like "roller derby," except that the players attempt to injure or even kill one another for the sake of the crowd.

One of the *Rollerball* players becomes too popular for the Board of Directors to tolerate; they can't retire him because of this popularity, so they decide to injure him. This doesn't work because he is a superior player and his team keeps winning games. Finally, the Board decides to cancel all rules of the game and plans to have a competitor team assassinate him. This doesn't work; the player, Jonathan, kills everyone who is involved in this plot and the crowd is quite pleased and overthrows the Board. The meaning from the movie is clear: one cannot destroy individualism. The message to the moviegoer is that out-of-control corporations cannot survive; individuals and their contributions are still very much needed. The stage is always set for the destruction of collectivism.

A similar dichotomy exists in *Platoon* (1967). The strict parent role (Sgt. Barnes) is a staff sergeant who fights the war "by the book," who is quick to shoot peasants who may or may not be the enemy, and who emphasizes chain of command at all times. The other equally ranking sergeant (Sgt. Elias) is supportive of team members, serves as a moral model for his men, who risks his own life to save that of comrades-in-arms. Sgt. Barnes views the Army as a well-oiled machine doing what it is designed to do, i.e., obliterate the enemy. Sgt. Elias views the Army as a collection of individuals with fears, hopes, and other human traits that can be used in a positive manner to accomplish its mission without violating the Geneva Convention. The main character, a private who is swayed by both points of view, finally realizes that people in general are swayed by both types of leaders. He states in the script that we all have two fathers, a "systems" father and a humane father; we spend a portion of our organizational lives deciding which to emulate.

The points in the movie parallel those made by Likert, Argyris, Blake & Mouton, Hersey-Blanchard, Lakoff and MacGregor. Although all of these theorists have a leading toward the "humane" father, the movie will, to some extent, encourage the I/O Psychologist to diagnose the kind of client culture being encountered and, of most importance, either attempt to "live" with it or attempt to install organizational change. Most models today would push us towards the nurturing parenting, but one still has to determine whether the energy required for a change would actually be within the organization's capabilities.

Pearl Buck's *The Good Earth* is about the transition of Chinese culture from dynastic to socialist. It is called a "psychological novel" because it is an investigation of psychological topics and argues that personality can change as do organizational and cultural factors in one's environment.

Rolvaag's book, *Giants in the Earth,* is a study of how the cultural depravation of pioneer society in the Midwest can have severe effects on mental health. The two novels, both Nobel Prize winners, are testimonies to persons faced with overwhelming odds against their psychological survival as human beings.

A final note in this chapter is about the value of arts and sciences, language studies, aesthetics, etc., for the I/O Psychologist. It is likely that someone who concentrates solely on technology may miss out on insights that can strengthen values, provide for cultural understanding, and shed light on the nature of philosophical views. For example, a well-known organizational psychologist made the comment in a training program that "we know a lot about conflict, having studied it for 40 years or more." The truth is that, although organizational development has focused on conflict management, conflict itself has been a topic of human learning for a long time. Roman and Greek philosophers, leaders of the Enlightenment and many others have had much to say about how to predict, understand, alleviate, and also aggravate human conflict. Modern psychologists have done much to reduce conflict, but they certainly didn't do the original thinking on this subject.

An example of egotism on our part is the operational definition of the idea of "meaning in life." The *American Psychologist* recently hosted an article on "meaning" in which the concept itself was defined empirically by a carefully constructed measure of "meaning" (Heinselman, et al). The authors didn't take into consideration the fact that "meaning" (the word) defies definition. Saying one has meaning in life can express hundreds of different feelings, religious beliefs, ideas, values, personality concepts, etc.; one could argue that the concept itself is not subject to definition. It may be that individuals create meaning through work and that job satisfaction, performance, and motivation are related to meaning. One would still have to come up with an operational definition of what meaning is, however, and this may be beyond psychometrics. The study of meaning should be left in the hands of the philosophers; psychologists can benefit from reading about such broad concepts but to call them science is misleading.

Hopefully, I/O psychology can gain greater insights into the very societies it is attempting to improve by gaining a better grasp of the artistic, literary, and aesthetic communities and their activities and products.

18. Business Ethics

As we look over business practices in general, it seems that most companies treat their stockholders, employees, and customers well. However, there are a significant number of corporations and similar entities that have questionable ethics with respect to these audiences. Some of them may attempt to force the consultant to violate his own ethical code in order to assist in implementing sour practices. Generally, the causative factor is the company's maximization of financial gain while, at the same time, de-emphasizing the job satisfaction and "human" needs of workers, staff, managers, and customers such as have been described by Maslow, Herzberg, Hersey/Blanchard and McGregor. The current chapter is devoted to business ethics and, the next, to ethics for psychologists. Before we proceed on either topic, however, we should cover a moral background for both.

In a paper presented by Lefkowitz, et.al., at a 2004 SIOP conference, the authors challenge the I/O profession to look at its own values: "It is the profession's core values that both anchor and trigger the virtues expected of its members." Lefkowitz and other discussants point to our veneration of the scientist-practitioner model and the fact that it fails to echo the moral perspective represented by the humanistic/beneficial tradition in psychology. In a world in which technocratic professions have emerged such as the systems analyst, the marketing specialist, the public relations expert, or the engineering technologist, there is an absence of altruism or service mentality characteristic of established professions such as medicine, law, the ministry, or teaching. There is no real attempt to articulate moral standards in occupations such as the earlier ones mentioned.

Where in this dichotomy should I/O psychology lie? Is it a traditional profession or a technocratic one? Some psychologists argue that one should check values at the door to be a credible scientist. The question, however, is still open—is a moral compass needed to direct the goals to which the science is applied? One argument states that the "value free assumption" is not merely neutral and is certainly not benign, but serves to mask the influence of a different and contradictory value system which prizes productivity, profitability, and shareholder value above all else. As psychologists and business partners with our clients, do we give up the obligation to inform them that their goals are not realistic and may cause employees to suffer if they are realized? The remainder of this chapter and the next are written in the spirit of Lefkowitz's paper and the self-examination it asks both of ourselves and our client organizations.

Several situations and cases will be described with respect to business ethics. They are not in any particular order.

1) Business Schools: There are ongoing disputes between liberal arts and business departments in university settings. One criticism of business departments/schools is that a student learns to be an entrepreneur and not a general businessperson. For example, at a couple of well-known business schools, it is taught that one should learn how to purchase an on-going enterprise, "grow" it to several times its initial value, and then sell it at a large profit when the market is right. Little consideration is given to the professional development of the employees; the technical innovations are seen as a source of profit rather than as a boost to technology. Under this model it is possible for an entrepreneur to have a successful business (ready for sale) without even knowing much about the products made or the processes used. The name of the game is becoming wealthy without worrying too much about whether the company contributes anything to society or how employees will fare once the business is sold. Imagine that someone has been with the company for 10 years and has really learned the business when he/she is now told to leave because of the business plan of the new buyer. Acquisitions often are attractive because of labor cost reductions which can be effected when companies are combined and redundant support personnel eliminated. However, mergers often fail....partially because of the stress of incompatibility of the cultures involved.

2) An order-by-computer seller with a number of warehouses across the country: Although the public may think that this is a very successful

enterprise, investigative reporting showed that a negative culture is very much present there (Hightower, Jim, *The Lowdowner*). Production is very much dominated by micro-systems designed by industrial engineers and accountants. People who work the inside jobs have so many seconds (calculated by company computers) to fill a given order and go on to the next one. If the work is not done on time, points are subtracted from their individual accounts until a limit is reached, at which point they are discharged. Other points are subtracted if a worker is one minute late from taking a 30-minute lunch break. All laborers are actually contractors and the company doesn't pay withholding, health benefits, or retirement benefits. It is, then, not complicated to terminate a worker. The company's warehouses are located in low employment areas and it is not difficult to maintain a labor force at the warehouse in spite of the frequent terminations that take place.

This case, then, is an example of a company weak in employee concern and sound labor practices. Much research in the I/O field shows that positive changes in employee practices would probably increase both morale and productivity. This company is well known for quick turnaround on orders taken; however, it is difficult to see how its labor practices can last indefinitely.

3) Pay discrepancies: The country now suffers from a huge discrepancy between executive compensation and that of the average worker. There are a number of studies showing this condition; for the purposes of illustration, here are some figures produced by one: A CEO in some companies could make as much as $100,000,000 annually while the average worker may have to settle for $45,000 annually. This is politically devastating, particularly when it can be shown that there is no relationship between CEO pay and earnings per share (*Business Week's Annual Survey of Executive Compensation*). This means that there is no relationship between the growth of the company and the amount paid to the CEO during the period of measurement. One of the mechanisms here is that the Board of Directors is selected for their reputation in the community and business in general and not for their experience in the industry. This was very sad

for Enron, whose Board apparently was not able to use critical thinking when looking at deals proposed by the president and the financial officials of the corporation.

4) Supporting the conventional wisdom: There are times, when under pressure from one partner or another (stockholders, employees, customers, etc.) an executive committee needs to have its strategies confirmed by an outside party. There are a few consultants who will affirm the "conventional wisdom" after they have been brought in to solve a problem. If the conventional wisdom is that the company wants to stay "lean and mean," then the consultant's report will say so and will offer examples of how the company can cut back (less capital expenditure, fewer employees, reduced supervisory force, a different approach to benefits, etc.). Data can be interpreted in different ways; in this example it may have been also possible that reducing personnel could have been an expensive hurdle to jump rather than a guarantee of cost savings. The point is that the overwhelming priority in this consulting approach is one of deciphering what the client wants and then giving it to them, thus reassuring good relations between client and consultant in the future and assuring repeat business.

5) Decisions made by wrong entity: In a particular plant on the Gulf Coast, many personnel decisions were made by the local head of Human Resources. Specifically, HR would decide on promotions, selection, discipline, and awards. This was caused by the philosophy of the East Coast executives of the company; the local person could be "trusted" to control people even when he only had a staff job. Local managers lived pretty much with the fear that their personnel preferences may not be respected and that the "wrong" person may receive the next key job. Local Operations and Maintenance Managers should be able to control their own operations. They would very likely choose someone qualified rather than someone whose major characteristic was loyalty to Headquarters.

6) Decisions made independent of knowledge of actual job performance: A particular "tall" organization had a number of subsidiaries and many levels of management. Assessment psychologists were used

to test candidates independent of actual performance; the chief executive did not trust performance appraisals done by immediate bosses within the hierarchy. The ultimate result was that the assessment became the *only* procedure that was used to promote. This led to an atmosphere in which actual performance was de-emphasized since the only thing that mattered was rating by an outside party (the psychologist).

7) Attitude survey subpoenaed by workers: In this case a very thorough attitude survey was subpoenaed in a class action lawsuit. The weaknesses of the company personnel policies and actions were shown in the survey, but they were written for the company and not for viewing by the workers except when the company had a chance to respond to them (survey feedback technique). The author was angered by this subpoena because the company was responding to the survey results and improving practices of all sorts; the survey was never intended to be given to workers without a feedback procedure. This, of course, is an example of worker aggression rather that business ethics, but the thinking here is parallel. The point is that occasionally worker groups themselves are the cause of organizational negativity.

8) Collusion between client and consultant: This involves another type of collusion similar to that discussed above in point #4. This one involves science on the part of the consultant and judgment on the part of the client. I/O Psychologists often write and have publishers produce tests they have written, standardized, and validated against a criterion. Along with ability and knowledge tests, there is a current trend to publish tests of personality, work habits, and work motivations. These attempt to measure human traits on various scales or indicators including "conscientiousness," "detail-orientation," "energy," "assertiveness," "sales orientation," etc. Hundreds of these tests and trait measurement devices have been created over a lengthy period of time. A variety of methods of construction have been used, including so-called "rational' methods, factor analysis, the method of known groups, item response theory, etc. Test or scale writers can attempt to measure a large variety of human characteristics. Some of the scales created or used are questionable in terms of what is being

measured by the scale. For example, if one creates a scale called "authoritarianism" and uses it to hire managers who are dogmatic and hypercritical, he/she is doing the organization and society a disservice. Authoritarianism is a pathological behavior which brings in managers who may not be fully mature and who may want to use power for self-enhancement. The "collusion" here is that both client and consultant are involved in a selection that moves the type of "new hire" toward someone who is dictatorial rather than someone who is rational.

9) Employee Engagement: A trait that will be discussed in line with #8 above is called "employee engagement." Although this is really a constellation of traits (Macey, 2012), it can be thought of as a scale that measures willingness to devote oneself to the employing organization. Implied in the psychological content of this scale is the concept that one can select job candidates who will give their "all" to the company, who might put the needs of the company ahead of obligations to self, family, community and even church or faith. If a number of persons scoring high on "engagement" were hired in the supervisory and management ranks, the company would have to function while being run by persons who may attempt to "get the job done at any cost" (especially human cost). From the perspective of lifestyle, this environment could easily cause maladjustment, frustration, and actually low productivity.

The psychologist pushing for the "engagement" approach to hiring would have to evaluate his/her own ethics since the professional product may be doing more harm than good. It is especially important that I/O psychologists not fall into the trap that what management wants is always good for individual workers. Early examples of this kind of thinking can be found in Henry Ford's concept of how one can take advantage of the average worker. He fought union sentiment, created the boredom associated with production line work, and ignored claims of mistreatment. Ford, in spite of his contributions to mass production, was a Nazi sympathizer at one point and may have toyed with fascist ideas about managing people.

Unfortunately, sometimes with modern psychology's blessing, new and subtler attempts to manipulate the work force have come to pass. The fact that these attempts can have a good face does not excuse them. With respect to subtly, some "modern" managers use Theory Y to begin a project but soon fall into a Theory X pattern of assumptions once the work is underway. These concepts of Douglas McGregor (1960) are still alive and well; unfortunately; the experience of the author is that Theory X managers still outnumber Theory Y.

Newman and Harrison (2008), in their article on employee engagement, present sample items from a variety of scales originally intended to measure the concept. The Utrecht Work Engagement Scale (Schaufeli & Bakker, 2003) was the latest development prior to those of today's contributors. It is worth a look at some of the items on the Utrecht Scale plus those assessing such topics as organizational commitment, job satisfaction, job effort, positive effect, and job involvement. A table in the Newman and Harrison article is entitled "Redundancy of Work Engagement Items with items from well-known Instruments." A partial list follows:

1) I find the work that I do full of meaning and purpose.
2) I am proud to tell others that I am part of this organization.
3) When I am working, I forget everything else.
4) I live, eat and breathe my job.
5) I get carried away when I am working.
6) Most of my interests are centered in my job.
7) It is difficult to detach myself from my job.
8) [Reverse scoring] I usually feel detached from my job.
9) At my work, I feel bursting with energy.
10) I am proud to tell others that I am part of this organization.
11) I am willing to put in a great deal of effort beyond that normally expected in order to help this organization succeed.
12) Sometimes I lie awake at night thinking about the next day's work.
13) At my work, I always persevere, even when things do not go so well.
14) [Reverse scoring] There's not much to be gained by sticking with this organization indefinitely.

It is apparent to the author that if such items are used to select or promote employees, the organization could contain more persons who are "addicted" to their jobs or to the culture in which they are present. One could surmise that organizations who demand commitment and who may not care about work-life balance may seek out such persons, expecting that they would tolerate autocratic leadership styles and an atmosphere of little support, little attention to interpersonal facilitation, little attention to morale, etc. Unfortunately, several large companies are like this. One of them was characterized to the author by a major manager there as a "meat grinder."

A Case Study in Organizational Analysis

The author was contacted by a current client because of possible difficulties in the MIS department. The client was a hospital pharmacy chain with more than 100 locations. The author had watched this chain grow and assignments had included managerial selection, surveys of local pharmacy managers, counseling of problem employees, and executive coaching. As the chain grew, new administrative methods evolved and the IT Department had grown considerably.

New technology was in the planning and experimental stage which would permit the mass re-ordering of drugs from major pharmaceutical houses on a cost-effective basis plus other programs such as the ordering of drugs on a daily basis for hospital patients. The new technology was behind in implementation and the executive committee wanted more information than the Department Manager had offered.

The author was called in by the vice-president of information systems and was asked what should be done. Together they decided that the consultant should do a few exploratory interviews for hypotheses about the cause of the problem. These interviews suggested that a broader base of information was needed. It turned out that the staff of a federal government contractor had been hired by the company a couple of years before because of their familiarity with the particular IT system that had already been chosen. The Department Manager had been on the federal contracting team.

Appointments were made with all supervisors, programmer/analysts, administrators, system analysts, and the Department Manager. Two psychologists pooled their interview results and a story and a pattern began to emerge. There were, of course, IT personnel who had been on board before the government personnel were brought in. Among other things, a "we-they" atmosphere had been forming. The Department Manager had effectively demoted the old regime and viewed them as non-productive. Actually, the old guard knew the system applications much better and were being short-circuited by the manager. When the manager was giving reports to the executive committee, everything sounded fine and the new applications were described as on schedule to be installed. However, the Vice President of Information Technology had been getting messages from inside people complaining about morale and communications. The interviews done by the consultants revealed that the manager was verbally abusive to the original group, was ignoring their work, and was socializing on and off the job with his "in-group." A confidential report written by the consulting team was read by the Vice President, and the Department Manager was fired the next week. Normally it is not preferable to let people go after an organizational analysis. However, in this case and as this person was attempting to create a good image with the executive committee, he was being toxic with subordinates and it did not appear that his approach to leadership could be tolerated anymore.

This is a case in organizational analysis rather than organizational development. Still, developmental goals were set for the remaining employees. Follow-up in a few months showed that people were doing developmental activities, that a new manager was hired, that morale was improved, and the system application had begun to function. The company was absorbed within a year by a large medical services firm and further follow-up was not possible.

Brief Summary

In summary, then, we have offered different types of situations in which one can make a strong argument for better business ethics, educational ethics, more thoughtful client/consultant collaboration, and more interaction between board-level or executive-level incumbents with the rest of the organization. We know that some business schools pay relatively little attention to ethics in their coursework and this should change. The next chapter will explore ethical and business behavior of individual practitioners.

19. DEVIATIONS FROM GOOD PRACTICE

Positive examples of psychological practice are more instructive than negative ones. This is true of many fields because the newcomer needs a model of what *to do* rather than what *not to do*. However, there are subtleties and complexities in our field that can encourage bad practice. Examples from actual practice are listed below; they are drawn either from consultant behavior observed by the author or from stories told to the author by reputable sources. They are not necessarily situations that have been attached to formal ethical principles as of yet; however, they could be in the future. There is no attempt here to criticize individuals; rather the situations are presented with ideas for how particular mistakes could have been avoided and how they can be better handled in the future.

The first group of deviations from good practice relate to project process and supervision.

1) **Decision-Making**: Some I/O's are good decision-makers but forget that their basic role on a team-building or O.D. project is to facilitate decision-making rather than actually make decisions. On a quantitative project, when the professional is collecting data, analyzing data, and reporting results, decisions and recommendations are of course appropriate. However, when client development is the task, it is not appropriate to make business decisions. In other words, the consultant should not focus on the operational task itself rather than on the human process of facilitating the client's doing the task and making the appropriate decisions.

2) **Evaluation of Professionals**: In some consulting firms, there is a tendency for senior psychologists to evaluate apprentices on profitability, billings, or administrative performance rather than on key professional behaviors such as judgment, client relations,

work approach, application of technology, etc. This, of course, offers no feedback on professional development and leaves the apprentice not knowing where to improve. Chapter 5 of this book outlines evaluation and feedback approaches for use with apprentice, journeyman, and managerial level psychologists. Also, sometimes it is forgotten that less experienced I/O's require OJT and not just academic coursework.

3) **Professional Disagreement**: Disagreeing with a project manager in front of the client can occur. Sometimes an argument will break out between psychologists and this damages client relationships. They should be handled in private; it is part of the job of the young psychologist to learn how to differ with a superior in a constructive manner.

4) **The Conventional Wisdom**: There have been a few I/O's who reinforce the local "conventional wisdom" rather than telling the client that there are things to worry about. There are several possible motives in so doing. One is that the consultant wishes to be known as having the same "wisdom" as does the inner circle. Another is that the consultant fears he will lose the client since he/she will be the bearer of bad news. It may be unethical, however, for the psychologist to ignore what she/he has actually learned from the situation.

5) **Root Cause Analysis**: We have offered examples of the need for "root cause analysis" in other chapters. It should be put in this list as well. If there is a need, then the analysis should be done. The client can only be hurt by not exploring what may be the source of the problem. If the consultant addresses only short-term, immediate factors, the client may never come to see the problem in perspective.

6) **Cause of the Problem**: Sometimes the I/O is tempted to claim that his/her techniques or approach will "solve" the client's problem rather than just address it. The client is not buying engineering services; the I/O can tell the client that the service is typically effective but should also state that it is not perfect because we are dealing with human behavior which is not subject to the precise measurements offered by chemistry or physics.

The next set of deviations from good practice than can occur are in the category of inappropriate and invalid professional behaviors.

7) **Seminars**: The first example here usually occurs during presentations and seminars. The basic problem is that a known professional and/or firm will lead a seminar on a stated topic without really getting into the pre-published learning objectives. The author has been to a seminar on supervisory training in which there were no real points made about how to test or train supervisors. To be sure, points were made about the results of training, about how many clients were using the particular system, and about the value of the program to the market in general. The author began to have the impression that anything proprietary was not going to be discussed or shown. Now, presenting on what a proprietary idea *is* can be a different topic than what one *does*. In other words, it should be possible to offer sample items, to show item derivation techniques, to offer segments from the training program, etc., without actually giving or donating the system to the persons attending the seminar. The firm offering this program could in fact "whet the appetite" of those attending, causing them to want to know more about their programs. Otherwise the firm is simply making PR points about their product. An educational seminar or workshop is not the occasion to actively sell one's products, ideas, or packaged programs.

8) **Overuse of Proprietary Programs or Instruments**: Some of us have spent a lot of time and trouble building a program or technique, and we wish to reclaim investment plus make profits. The difficulty here is that the technique may be repeatedly pushed onto and used by clients regardless of whether it fits their problem(s) or not. An example here would be firms who claim to be general consultants but who publish one or two instruments and who invariably use them in a project. They also shape every project into one that appears to be approachable with the one or two instruments. This is clearly in service of the instrument rather than the project. In the case of computerized test batteries, it is often the case that the motive of the principal is to sell the computerized testing model rather than to match job with predictor.

9) **Format over Substance**: There are consulting firms who contract with psychologists in the field to perform and write reports on psychological assessments under the "brand" name of the firm. Often these firms require that the assessment be written in a standard format. Psychologists at the headquarters location edit the reports to make sure they follow the standard format, often without reference to the "substance" of the report. This is a real problem for the report writers, who begin to feel that the "branded" firm is more concerned with format than with substance. The editors may suggest that every interpretative statement in the report consist of a behavioral finding, how this finding helps or hurts organizational function, and what can be done to improve the behavior or to capitalize on it. The contracting psychologist is not really free to provide a major interpretation of test/interview results, to focus on how the "finding" may have developed over a period of time, or to provide a realistic personal development pattern based on the assessment as a whole rather than on each "piece" of it. Following the required format results in a choppy, piecemeal, non-integrated assessment which deprives the client of receiving the benefits of a full psychological evaluation.

10) **Coaching**: Often I/O's are asked to "coach" managers and executive staff as individuals. The process is usually devoted toward helping the subject to deal with "blockages" in the personal, interpersonal, and organizational arenas. Goal-setting is a dominant type of intervention in these sessions; also counseling techniques are used to help the subject with self-improvement. The process, in total, is designed to help her/him become a better manager. There are companies and situations, however, in which coaches are subtly instructed to help the individual accept a negative corporate culture. The persons being coached are assisted in tolerating a dysfunctional culture. In effect, persons being coached are told "Look, there's nothing you can do to change the organization. It's best to learn how to grin and bear it." Jill McMillan, author of the article "Organizational Codependency," has performed an excellent job of describing how cultures take a turn for the worst and how they can be returned to the path of normalcy. Asking people to accept a negative culture is not one of

them. The originators of corporate coaching believed that it should help people improve themselves in order to achieve a positive rather than negative culture.

11) **Inappropriate Role**: Through professional circles, the author knew of a psychologist who was performing individual assessments on the managerial population of a middle-sized petrochemical company. He was with a reputable firm, but one that moved in and out of giving business advice along with personal development advice. The firm was known to perform lengthy interviews and to go into personal, educational, and career history to some depth. The twist in this story is that the psychologist actually became an employee a few months later. He was now Manager of Human Resources and would have access to the assessment files that he and his firm had created as psychologists. It is not difficult to grasp the point that someone who had a lot of confidential information concerning the managers assessed was now one of their bosses. His new position would give him a lot to say about their careers, assignments, and terminations. Also, the assessment data was collected under psychologist ethics, and the subjects being evaluated were not told that the psychologist ethics (confidentiality, etc.) no longer applied. This case should be in the ethics manual; it is clearly a violation of confidentiality and other ethical principles. It seems to the author that the ultimate dysfunction here was the professional climate that had gradually swept over the psychologist's firm. They may have experienced a certain ease in exerting power in the petrochemical firm and thought it entirely appropriate for one of their own to take on the new job.

The following cases are examples of non-psychologists taking on professional roles:

12) **Verbally Skilled Non-Professionals**: It has happened that people with a degree in a related field who are verbally sharp and personable have been given roles in important work. The project manager may have felt that verbal skills were important because many I/O's are data-driven and not people-driven. This does not work, of course,

because verbosity doesn't substitute for professional skills. The answer here is practice and experience for qualified professionals rather than substituting for them with individuals who can express themselves well.

13) **Non-Psychologist Owners**: Occasionally, a psychological consulting firm is purchased by a non-psychologist. This violates the law for forming Professional Corporations (P.C.'s) in most states. Also it sends a message to the client that I/O skills that have been vigorously developed are not really needed; that any sharp businessperson can run a psychology firm. When a psychologist is directly supervised by a non-psychologist the same situation occurs. Again, the field is damaged and becomes non-viable as a profession.

14) **Practicing without a License**: An I/O who is unlicensed by his/her state of practice may venture into professional territory that clearly requires a license. The use of projective and well-developed personality tests as well as "clinical" interviews requires that the psychologist be licensed. The APA ethics manual clearly applies to I/O psychologists as well as clinical and educational psychologists. Often, however, I/O's do not feel the need for a license because most of their work is statistical or "systems" related.

15) **Marketing**: If a marketing specialist is hired to sell psychological services, we have a similar problem. In the first place, the "salesman" has only a limited understanding of what she/he is selling. In the second place, the first contact between client and consultant is actually a professional one. If the potential client begins to discuss the situation in his organization, this is actually the first step in the consulting process. Confidential or private information may be revealed which the listener has to treat within the bounds of her/his ethics code. A marketing specialist is certainly not trained to handle sensitive information that he may pick up.

We have, then, covered a number of deviations from standard practice above. It is important to discuss them because often the practitioner is confronted with a situation without precedent in his/her practice and he/she is truly undecided about the ethics involved. The reader will have some capsule of the author's collection of experience along these lines. The idea here is to shed some light on the possibility that members of the field may be sliding into unacceptable territory and may benefit from a colleague's point of view. This is not to say that the colleague is perfect; we all will benefit from feedback that reminds us of the ethics and what we can do in a constructive fashion. Further guidelines about ethics are documented in Lowman (2006).

20. Being in a Psychological Practice; Integration of Chapters

Much of the book has already covered I/O practice from the point of view of projects attempted. There is something to be said, however, about life in the practice itself. The author has worked in the context of small, medium, and large firms and, of course, would have different things to say about each. Probably the best thing to discuss is what happens within each type and why it is important for one to "match up" with the best fit for him/herself. In small firms, the professional will have a broad perspective over projects and will have more responsibilities up and down the task ladder. He/she may make coffee at one minute and greet an executive to discuss a project the next. As this book points out, he/she is likely to be a general practitioner and probably has no more than one or two partners or associates. A list of psychologists is kept for use on larger projects on a contract basis. Partnership disputes can happen, but, based on the author's experience, they are more likely to occur in legal, engineering, and medical practices than in psychological practices.

When they do occur, the issues usually include whether people should be licensed, what kinds of personalities do clients prefer, whether a partner has specialized knowledge in a high volume activity such as individual assessment, management training, legal aspects of selection and promotion, organization development, etc. Sometimes a partnership is actually enhanced if the partners are different types of personalities (one may be introverted and bury themselves in data while the other may very client-centered, extroverted, interactive, etc.).

In medium-sized firms, things are similar, but there is usually a competition among the principals for "worker" psychologists. If one gets along with a particular principal, he/she is likely to work with that person more often. Some firms are interdisciplinary in nature and have industrial engineers,

MBA's, market researchers, finance experts, etc. It is interesting to watch an I/O psychologist work with an industrial engineer. The engineer is not trained in such areas as observer effect, obtaining rapport with workers, social factors in productivity, etc. The psychologist is not trained in time and motion study, manufacturing methods improvement, production statistics, etc.

In large consulting firms, specialists reign supreme and psychologists eventually become administrators. These firms have the depth to take on a multitude of large projects and have Fortune 100 companies, large police and fire departments, government agencies, and the military as clients. It is basically not cost-effective for them to take on small projects. Often they cover overhead by selling products as well as services including tests, programs, types of organizational intervention, etc. Some of these firms are huge in size and often are multidimensional in nature.

We have looked mostly at roles played by psychologists employed in consulting firms. Those who work in corporations, government, academia, and other organizations have not been explored on a case-by-case basis. This is largely because the author has not been an employee of any such group, although he has worked with all of them from time to time on a contract basis. The roles can be very different because "inside" people have a boss to please and it is difficult for them to do "root cause analysis" when that person or his colleagues are in fact "part of the problem." Internal psychologists must be willing to take risks to work on "root causes." An outside professional usually has 10-15 ongoing clients and losing one of them is not devastating, so he/she can get at root causes.

The author at one time was considering engineering as a profession and, later, medicine. Neither of these worked out, and it wasn't until he was studying psychology that something became clear. He was very absorbed in science and technology, as would be reflected in engineering and medicine. However, he was also very absorbed in social and humanitarian endeavors as one would find in sociology, psychology and anthropology. This "finding" was confirmed by one of the major work interest tests that he took at age twenty-six or so. Psychology is a mixture of science and social interest; the other two more or less ignore social science and the author has been very satisfied with his ultimate career choice.

Integration

It is important at this time to make some integrative statements about the themes in the book. I have attempted to show by case study and quantitative and qualitative analysis many of the client situations that could be brought to a general practitioner and what could be done to address them. I have also attempted to show by example some of the ethical and problematic dilemmas that could occur in the course of daily consulting practice. Always, sometimes in the background, are the choices that have to be made between quantitative and qualitative approaches, between theory and practice, between subjective and objective, and between art and science. Developing a design for a project is often a very thought-filled process, as is coping with mid-stream difficulties. It is a very rich field to *work* in, and there are many opportunities for job satisfaction, even when compromises have to be made between high quality and medium quality outcomes.

There is truth in all social disciplines including literature, drama, sociology, anthropology. It is important that the I/O Psychologist avoid turning his/her back on any of them. The model of leadership drawn from the movie, *Platoon*, for example, rivals those brought forth by Lakoff or Blake and Mouton. The understanding of organizational culture drawn by Terrance Deal (1982) rivals some of those coming from organizational development. The idea of qualitative research leads us into valid inquiry of some of the human processes that are different to quantify with "equal interval" data.

So what is the book really about? Is it more or less a collection of cases in which techniques were applied? Is there a "core" meaning to the field which we should not overlook? The author believes that there *is* a core of human service concerns that infiltrates, if you will, all projects. For applied psychology, the question remains one of, given a need or problem in an organization, can the techniques as put together by the practicing psychologist truly assist in the achievement of corporate objectives while advancing the welfare of individual employees at the same time?

It may be that the answer to the question will depend on the core values of the particular psychologist. If, for example, his/her core values are centered around the maximization of sales and the minimization of costs, it is less likely that he/she will devote attention to employee well-being. If one focuses on profit alone, often they will be disappointed because, after Likert, the path to profitability is often one of focusing on "intervening variables" (employee involvement, job satisfaction, employee well-being, etc.). For this psychologist, the meaning of the work is found in the development and well-being of both the organization and the individual.

21. REFERENCES

American Psychological Association (APA). (2002). Ethical Principles of Psychologists and Code of Conduct. Retrieved from *http://www.apa.org/ethics/code/index.aspx.*

Argyris, Chris. *Integrating the Individual and the Organization.* New York, NY, Wiley, 1964.

Berne, Eric. A New and Effective Method of Group Therapy. *American Journal of Psychotherapy,* 12: 735-743, 1958.

Blake, R., and Mouton, J. *The Managerial Grid: The Key to Leadership Excellence.* Houston, Gulf Publishing Co., 1985.

Blakeney, Roger; Broenen, Robert; Dyck, John; Frank, Blake; Glenn, Dana; Johnson, Doug; Mayo, Clyde. Implications of the Results of a Job Analysis of I/O Psychologists. *The Industrial Psychologist (TIP),* April, 2004.

Bolles, Richard N. *What Color is Your Parachute?* Berkeley: Ten Speed Press, 2014.

Buck, Pearl S. *The Good Earth,* New York: Simon and Schuster, 1938.

Campion, James E. Work Sampling for Personnel Selection. *Journal of Applied Psychology,* 56, 40-44.

Campion, M.A.; Campion, J. E.; Hudson, J. P. Structured Interviewing: A Note on Incremental Validity and Alternative Question Types. *Journal of Applied Psychology,* 76, 897-908.

Cascio, Wayne F. *Applied Psychology in Human Research Management,* Longman Higher Education, 1987.

Christal, R. E. and Weissmueller, J. Job Task Inventory Analysis. In G. Gael (Ed.) *The Job Analysis Handbook for Business, Industry, and Government.* New York: Volume II, 1036-1050, Wiley, 1988.

Deal, Terrence and Kennedy, Allan. *Corporate Cultures: The Rites and Rituals of Corporate Life.* 1982

Equal Opportunity Employment Commission, Civil Service Commission, Department of Labor and Department of Justice (1978). Uniform Guidelines on Employee Selection Procedures. *Federal Register,* 43, 38295-38309.

Flanagan, J.C. The Critical Incident Technique. *Psychological Bulletin,* 51, 327-58.

Fleishman, Edwin A. *Studies in Personnel and Industrial Psychology.* Homewood, Illinois, Dorsey Press, 1967.

French, Wendel L, *Organization Development.* Toledo, Ohio: Hippo Books, 1988.

Gordon Personal Profile Inventory. Minneapolis: NCS Pearson, Inc., 2006.

Guion, Robert. *Assessment, Measurement, and Prediction for Personnel Decisions.* New York: Routledge Publishing, 2011.

Harrington, B. & Hall, D.T. *Career Management and Work-Life Integration,* Thousand Oaks, California, Sage, 2007.

Heintzelman, Semantha and King, Laura. Life is Pretty Meaningful. *Journal of the American Psychological Association,* v. 69, 6, 561-575.

Hersey, Paul; Blanchard, Kenneth; Johnson, Dewey. *Management of Organizational Behavior.* Englewood Cliffs, N. J.: Prentice Hall, 2014 (10th edition).

Hightower, Jim. *The Hightower Lowdown.* Austin: Public Intelligence.

The Industrial/Organizational Psychologist (TIP). A publication of the Society for Industrial/Organizational Psychologists, Inc. Washington, D.C.

Jeanneret, Richard. *The Position Analysis Questionnaire (PAQ),* Bellinghan, WA, PAQ Services. 1971.

Kesey, Ken. *One Flew Over the Cuckoo's Nest.* New York: Viking Press, 1962.

Lakoff, George. *Moral Politics.* Chicago: University of Chicago Press, 2002.

Lefkowitz, Joel, Moderator, "The Values of Industrial-Organizational Psychology: Who are We?" Panel Discussion, Annual Conference of the Society for Industrial and Organizational Psychology, Chicago, April, 2004.

Likert, Rensis. *New Patterns of Management.* New York: McGraw Hill, 1961.

Lowman, Rodney L., Editor, *The Ethical Practice of Psychology in Organizations* (2nd Edition), The American Psychological Assn., Washington DC, 2006.

Macey, Wm. and Schneider, B. The Meaning of Employee Engagement. *Industrial and Organizational Psychology.* 1, 2008, 3-30.

Mager, Robert. *Making Instruction Work.* Belmont, CA: Lake Publishing Co., 1988.

Maslow, Abraham. A Theory of Human Motivation. *Psychological Review.* 50, 370-396.

McGregor, Douglass. *The Human Side of Enterprise.* New York: McGraw-Hill, (1960).

McMillan, Jill J. Organizational Co-Dependency: The Creation and Maintenance of Closed Systems. *Management Communications Quarterly.* 9, 6-45.

Miller, Arthur. *Death of a Salesman.* Director: Volker Schlondorff, CBS. Made for Television, 1985.

Miller, Neal. *Learning and Motivation.* New York: Barnes and Noble, 1997.

Newman, Daniel and Harrison, David. Been There Bottled That: Are State and Behavioral Work Engagement New and Useful Construct Wines? *Industrial and Organizational Psychology.* 31-36, 2008.

The Office. Reveille and Universal, NBC Television; TV Series by Daniels, Greg. (2005-2013).

Peter, Laurence J. *The Peter Principle: Why Things Always Go Wrong.* New York: Wm Morrow & Co., 1969.

Rogers, Carl. A theory of Therapy, Personality, and Interpersonal Relationships as Developed in the Client-Centered Relationship. In (ed.) S. Koch, *Psychology: A study of Science, Vol. 3, Formulation of the Person and the Social Context.* New York: McGraw Hill, 1959.

Rollerball. Jewison, Norman (dir.). London. United Artists (1975).

Rolvaag, Ole E. *Giants in the Earth.* Currently offered by the Norwegian-American Historical Association, Northfield, MN, 1927.

Sheth, V. *Industrial Engineering and Practices.* Rennam, MI: Rennam Int'l Publishing, 2000.

Smith, P. C. and Kendall, L. M. Retranslation of expectations: An Approach to the Construction of Unambiguous Anchors for Rating Scales. *Journal of Applied Psychology.* 47, 457-460.

The Solomon Report. Petroleum Refinery Benchmarking Concepts. Toronto: Suncor Energy, 2009.

Stone, Oliver. *Platoon.* Film produced by Arnold Kopelson of Herndale Film Corp. Distributed by Orion Pictures, 1967.

Supervisory Profile Index, ePredix, a CEB company.

Wechsler, David. *Wechsler Adult Intelligence Scale* (4th ed.). New York: Pearson Education Corp (Psych. Corp), 2008.

Zedeck, Sheldon. *The Law School Admission Project: Looking Beyond the LSAT.* Berkeley: Berkeley Institute for Research on Labor and Employment, 2006.